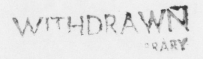

Caius Marius

a tragedy
by Richard Penn Smith

EDITED AND WITH AN INTRODUCTION BY

NEDA McFADDEN WESTLAKE

Philadelphia
University of Pennsylvania Press

COPYRIGHT © 1968 BY THE TRUSTEES OF
THE UNIVERSITY OF PENNSYLVANIA

LIBRARY OF CONGRESS CATALOG CARD NUMBER: 68-21553

7571

PRINTED IN THE UNITED STATES OF AMERICA

to the memory of

ARTHUR HOBSON QUINN,

a lover of American drama.

Acknowledgments

The dedication of this book to the memory of Arthur Hobson Quinn is an acknowledgment of a personal friendship and of his pioneer accomplishments in the history of American drama. When I first planned this work, I told him that I wished to dedicate it to him. Reflectively, he uttered the phrase I have used in the dedication, for which I found no substitute.

It is a pleasure to express my gratitude to other persons and institutions who have aided in this work. I am deeply indebted to Professor Sculley Bradley's knowledge of American drama and the literature of the period. His critical editorial judgment and his encouragement are sincerely appreciated. I am obligated to Professors Thomas C. Cochran and Hennig Cohen who also read the manuscript and to Professor William C. McDermott for special counsel on Roman history.

Others who have written on Richard Penn Smith and Edwin Forrest have given generously of their time and experience, particularly Dr. Richard Moody, Dr. Thomas Ollive Mabbott, and Dr. Bruce McCullough.

Mr. William Anderson at the Library and Museum of the Performing Arts, New York Public Library in Lincoln Center, has kindly provided research facilities from that rich collection. Special appreciation is due to the Princeton University Library, the Beinecke Library at Yale University, the Houghton Library at Harvard University, the Historical Society of Pennsylvania and the American Antiquarian Society.

Thayer Westlake's painstaking proofreading and interest in the subject have been most helpful. Mrs. Doris Sklaroff deserves sincere gratitude for her skill in typing and composition.

This work is published with the permission of the Library of the University of Pennsylvania for whose fine collection of American drama and related works I have been continuously grateful.

Contents

List of Illustrations

Caius Marius

Introduction

T
HE tragedy of *Caius Marius,* by Richard Penn Smith, was produced at the Arch Street Theatre in Philadelphia on Wednesday, January 12, 1831. With Edwin Forrest playing the famous Roman, the drama was repeated the following Friday, and the author's benefit performance was given on Monday, January 17. Forrest presented the play in New York, Boston, and again in Philadelphia in the fall of 1831. Apparently *Caius Marius* did not appear again until 1858, when Forrest gave permission for two performances in Philadelphia as a memorial to the author.

This meager record of performances, not unusual for new plays of the period, would seem to have little theatrical significance. However, by contemporary accounts the play was judged the *chef d'oeuvre* of Richard Penn Smith, an eminent Philadelphia lawyer, who had nine plays produced in the three years prior to *Caius Marius.* Edwin Forrest was the rising star of the American stage, who selected this tragedy as one of the eight native American dramas worthy of a substantial prize and attendant production. Only tantalizing fragments of the play were printed, and in spite of diligent search by theatrical historians, the manuscript did not come to light until 125 years after the first performance.

Richard Penn Smith was thirty-two when this play was first presented. In the third generation of a patrician family, living comfortably and unostentatiously as a practicing lawyer, he wrote ten more plays and published a novel and a collection of short stories in the next five years.[1]

[1] The best bibliography of Richard Penn Smith is in Sabin's *Bibliotheca Americana,* nos. 83 777-83 788, and in Bruce McCullough's doctoral thesis (University of Pennsylvania), *The Life and Writings of Richard Penn Smith with a Reprint of His Play, "The Deformed"* (Menasha, Wis., Banta, 1917). The appendix provides a list of Smith's dramatic works, with their dates of production and revival performances, location of manuscript when known, imprint, and sources when identified.

He was one of an energetic and fluid group that in the 1820's and 1830's was producing a climate of literary change and achievement in Philadelphia. The authors derived their ideas from European writers, but they sustained a native quality that would have a lasting effect on American letters. He was an intimate friend or an acquaintance of the playwrights James N. Barker, Robert Montgomery Bird, Robert T. Conrad, and David Paul Brown, the actors Edwin Forrest and William E. Burton, and the journalists Louis A. Godey, Joseph C. Neal, and Morton Mc-Michael. Writing of this group, Smith's son, Horace W. Smith, said, "Of all that intellectual coterie *my* father's star was the brightest, his wit the gayest, and his sarcasm the most cutting."[2]

Richard Penn Smith was the grandson of a brilliant, aggressive, opinionated, and dedicated clergyman and educator, William Smith, who became the first Provost of the College, Academy and Charitable School (the University of Pennsylvania) in 1755 at the age of twenty-eight. Dr. Smith had no direct influence on his grandson, who was only four years old when his grandfather died in 1803 at the age of seventy-six. However, Dr. Smith had well established the tradition of learning and literary achievement. His published sermons and writings on education and political issues were voluminous, and his varied exertions for the College were imaginative and untiring.[3]

William Moore Smith, born in 1759, was the oldest child of Dr. Smith and the father of Richard Penn Smith. He "was a gentleman of polished education and a poet of considerable reputation in his day."[4] *Poems on Several Occasions* . . . . (Philadelphia, 1786) is the only published volume by the father of the playwright, but the belletristic inclination was inherited by his son.

[2]Horace W. Smith, *Life and Correspondence of the Reverend William Smith, D.D.* (Philadelphia, George, 1879), II, 529.

[3]For biographical data, *cf.* Horace W. Smith, *Life and Correspondence of the Reverend William Smith, D.D.* (2 vols. Philadelphia, George, 1879). The most complete bibliography is Thomas R. Adams, *Trial Check List of the Writings of William Smith, First Provost of the University of Pennsylvania* (Philadelphia, 1950). Evidence of Dr. Smith's efforts in obtaining financial support for the University is in *The Collection Books of Provost Smith*, with Introduction by Jasper Yeates Brinton and Neda M. Westlake (Philadelphia, University of Pennsylvania Press [c.1964]).

[4]Henry Simpson, *The Lives of Eminent Philadelphians* (Philadelphia, Brotherhead, 1859), p. 899.

Philadelphia was the capital and national metropolis when Richard Penn Smith was born on March 13, 1799, at his father's home at the southeast corner of Fifth and Chestnut Streets. This residence remained the town house for the family for several years, but the boy must have spent much time at his grandfather's country estate. Provost Smith was indefatigable in securing funds for his College, but he was not one to overlook opportunities for the purchase of property advantageous to himself and his family. In the late 1760's Dr. Smith purchased a large tract of land near the Falls of the Schuylkill, and on the high hill south of the present Midvale Avenue and east of Ridge Avenue he built a mansion which was occupied by four generations of the Smith family, from 1774 to 1891.[5] The eighteen-room dwelling was called "Smith's Folly" by contemporaries because it was so far from the center of Philadelphia. However, by the time Richard Penn Smith was of school age, there was a grammar school at the Falls of the Schuylkill which the boy attended until he was ten. He and his brother had a tutor for their early classical training, and later they attended a small, privately owned school in Mt. Airy. In his adolescence, he was sent to Huntingdon on the Juniata River in south-central Pennsylvania, where his family had connections, and placed under the tutelage of a Presbyterian minister well known as a successful teacher of Greek and Latin.[6] In 1818 he returned to Philadelphia to study for the law.

The young man chose for his mentor William Rawle, then at the height of his diversified and productive career. Rawle, with Loyalist inclinations during the Revolution, had gone to England for legal training in the Middle Temple. However, he returned to his birthplace and was admitted to the bar in Philadelphia in 1783. His subsequent career, until his death in 1836 at the age of seventy-seven, was a brilliant succession of accomplishments.[7] Richard Penn Smith could have chosen no preceptor more distinguished or accomplished.

[5] Unpublished memorandum, National Parks Commission (1962), copy in University of Pennsylvania Library.

[6] Horace W. Smith, *op. cit*, II, 526.

[7] *Cf.* the summation of Rawle's life in the *Dictionary of American Biography*, Vol. XV.

In 1822, Smith interrupted his legal career to purchase the *Aurora* from William Duane.[8] This had been the most powerful Jeffersonian paper from the time Duane took over the editorship on the death of Benjamin Franklin Bache in 1798. Duane's vigorous assaults on the Federalists made him indispensable to the Democrats and contributive to the election of Jefferson in 1800. When he retired from the *Aurora* in 1822 to travel in South America, the paper seemed an attractive opportunity to Smith, an ardent Democrat. However, after five years, he found editorial responsibilities too burdensome and returned to the practice of the law. Nevertheless, the editorial experience was invaluable when he turned to the writing of fiction and drama for a period of literary productivity that was compressed between 1828 and 1835. In his later years, he was interested in educational and civic affairs. However, with an inheritance and an earned competence, he could afford semiretirement at the family estate his grandfather had built at the Falls of the Schuylkill, where he died in 1854 at the age of fifty-five.

The artist and his creative career reached a high point on the bitterly cold night in 1831 when Edwin Forrest gave his impassioned reading of Smith's interpretation of the life of the Roman tyrannical hero. Of the author's other nineteen plays, nine were produced before this tragedy, five afterward, and there were five incomplete or unproduced.[9] Three of the dramas were based on American historical events: the great naval battle at Plattsburg in the War of 1812, Jackson's victory at New Orleans in 1815, and William Penn's first interview with the Indians. Two were dramatizations of James Fenimore Cooper's novels, *The Water Witch* and *The Bravo*. English or French plays or stories were the inspiration for eight of the plays, light comedies or melodramas. *Caius Marius* was the only blank-verse tragedy written by Smith and the only one based on a classical theme, which the author had thoroughly explored and shaped to his dramatic purpose.

Caius Marius was born in a rustic Italian village in 157 B.C. By military accomplishment he rose successively through political

[8] *Cf. Ibid*, Vol. IV, for data on the career of William Duane.
[9] *Cf.* pp. 142-43 for the derivation of plays that have been identified.

offices until he gained his first consulship in 107, in his fiftieth year, and ousted his patron, Metellus, from the command of the campaign to subdue Jugurtha in Numidia, a northern province in Africa roughly coextensive with present eastern Algeria. Numidia had been allied with Rome from 206 B.C., and its rulers had enjoyed Roman favor and protection. Jugurtha, an illegitimate grandson of Masinissa, king of Numidia, had put to death his cousins, the co-heirs to the kingdom, and in 118 B.C. made himself master of the territory. His attempt to break away from Roman authority and thus threaten Rome's strategic position in the Mediterranean precipitated Roman reprisals in 111 B.C. The long struggle was ended by Marius with the capture of Jugurtha and his death in a Roman dungeon after Marius' triumph in 104 B.C. After this victory, Marius was elected consul year after year and defeated the invaders of northern Italy, the Teutones in 102 B.C. and the Cimbri in 101. His successes were due in a large part to army reforms and to his demand for land grants to his veterans. His choice of political allies was not so fortunate; he lost his popularity and influence and traveled for some time in Asia. He returned to serve in the Social War in 90 B.C., but his military accomplishments were outdistanced by Sulla, who was given the coveted command against Mithridates, king of Pontus. The decision was challenged by friends of Marius, but Sulla, refusing to turn over the army to Marius, marched on Rome.

This first attack of a Roman army upon the capital, a revolutionary action provoked by an inept and vacillating home government, marked the beginning of the end of the Republic. Marius fled the city, pursued to the very ruins of Carthage by his enemies. In 87 B.C. he was recalled by the consul, Cinna, who sought advantage against the other consul, Octavius, by joining with the forces which Marius could still call to his standard. Octavius could not hold the soldiery of Rome against Cinna and Marius, who instituted a reign of death and terror against their opponents. Marius appointed himself to his seventh consulship but died a few days later in January, 86 B.C., at the age of seventy-one. Shortly thereafter, Sulla returned from the first Mithridatic campaign, only to initiate another holocaust of vengeance on a shattered and unorganized government. Thus the rivalry between Marius and Sulla was an integral cause of the end of the Republic.

For dramatic effect, Smith compressed events in the life of Marius, introducing him as the victorious general returning to Rome with the captured Jugurtha. Marius' successful campaigns against the invaders of northern Italy are assumed to have occurred before his return from North Africa. His Asian wanderings are omitted, and his downfall is caused by the arrival of Sulla's army at the gates of Rome, rather than by his own infirmities.

The American political and social climate was the background for the author's use of historical materials to create for his friend, Edwin Forrest, a compellingly tragic character clothed in a Roman toga but uttering words of Jacksonian independence and equality.

The turbulence and excitement of a democratic awakening were by no means limited to the American scene after the mid-1820's. Writers were finding fresh inspiration in a variety of democratic expressions that met enthusiastic responses from readers and theatre-goers. The revolt of South American countries against Spain, the Greek Revolution of 1829, and the French Revolution of 1830 were stimuli that produced some of the best drama of the period, as well as some of the short-lived spectaculars with no literary merit but with a satisfying display of patriotism against a background of the sounds of warfare and the sight of the conquering hero. In the United States, the election of Andrew Jackson in 1828 seemed to many the appropriate culmination of the long struggle against tyranny and oppression. Native writers, freeing themselves from European models, were discovering literary potential not only in the stirring events abroad but also in their own brief national consciousness, with President Jackson a new type of American hero. The strictly historical dramatization of the American experience had been popular from the time of the Revolution, but the memorable plays of this immediate period went beyond the stereotyped Indian or the tableaux of a victorious Washington. Democracy was in the air, and it added the dimension of the value of the individual to the patriotic ideal.

From 1820 through 1840, there were 429 plays by American authors that had their first production on the American or English stage.[10] Apart from the farces and obviously light entertainment, twenty plays were based on books by American authors or were actual dramatizations of them: eleven by James Fenimore Cooper, four by William Gilmore Simms, five by Robert Montgomery Bird, and ten by other authors. Ninety-six were on national and patriotic themes, with emphasis on colonization, Indian encounters, the Revolution and the War of 1812. The plays of this period that were memorable to their contemporary audiences and are still a part of American dramatic history, if no longer in current repertoires, were those that echoed more than chauvinism or provincialism. They were appeals to the democratic consciousness and in many ways helped to define it. John Augustus Stone's *Metamora* and Robert Montgomery Bird's *Oralloossa* dramatically expressed the latent sympathy for the American Indians who had heroically withstood earlier white invasions. Nathaniel Parker Willis' *Tortesa the Usurer* and Bird's *The Broker of Bogota* represented the democratic sympathy for the worthy person of low estate in conflict with the lords of power and privilege. Bird's *The Gladiator* dramatized the uprising of the Roman slaves, and David Paul Brown's *Sertorius* glorified Spanish revolt against Roman rule. Robert T. Conrad's *Jack Cade* turned back to the Kentish rebellion in 1450 against Henry VI to give democratic emphasis to the struggle of the common Englishman for equality of rights and protection. Richard Penn Smith's *Caius Marius* was a presentation of the last months in the life of a Roman tyrant, but the play in performance becomes a vehicle for praise of the man who rises from the ranks, who lives simply with his subordinates and fights for them as well as with them, and whose tragedy lies in his ultimate conviction that those whom he championed have at last turned against him.

An investigation of the author's sources and of the stages of the manuscript itself supply indispensable commentary on the final product.

Richard Penn Smith had had early and thorough training in the classics, certainly sufficient to have read *Plutarch's Lives* in the original, where the fullest account of Marius' career appears,

---

[10]This is an analysis from the exhaustive list of plays in Arthur Hobson Quinn's *A History of the American Drama from the Beginning to the Civil War* (2nd ed. New York, Crofts, 1946), pp. 426-97.

as well as Sallust, Strabo, Livy, and Frontinus who all refer to some aspect of his life. However, as Professor Mabbott suggested in his discussion of the newspaper printing of the last scene of the play which he discovered in the *Philadelphia Saturday News* for January 7, 1836,[11] it seems likely that he used the Langhorne translation of Plutarch, of which there was an American edition in 1822. This is the translation referred to in this introduction and in subsequent notes to the play itself.[12] Significant alterations from Plutarch which Smith made for dramatic effect are noted at appropriate places in the text of the play. For the present, it is sufficient to note that a love affair is introduced between a son of Marius and the daughter of Metellus, the patron of Marius. Plutarch mentions a Granius as stepson of Marius, but is probably in error. Metellus had no daughter as far as we know. In the play the famous younger Marius is ignored, perhaps because of the inevitable confusion of two characters with the same name. Sulpitius is given much larger scope as Marius' loyal lieutenant; actually he was murdered before Marius returned from exile. The ordeal of Marius at the site of ruined Carthage is greatly heightened; Martha, who is attested to only in the campaign against the Teutones, becomes a major character; and the author does not allow his hero to die miserably in bed but poisons him and Martha on stage as Sylla's troops charge the gates of Rome.

Smith had a fine library, indicating his varied interests. There is a record of the sale of his law books in 1856 two years after his death,[13] but unfortunately the catalogue of his belletristic volumes referred to in Professor McCullough's thesis[14] has not been located. McCullough summarizes, "Of his general library there were numerous works of biography, travel, history, and poetry, but by far the largest collection devoted to a single subject was that pertaining to the English drama, which contained

[11]Thomas Ollive Mabbott, "Richard Penn Smith's Tragedy of *Caius Marius*," *American Literature*, II,2 (May 1930), 142-56. The text printed in the newspaper varies from the manuscript by only two words, not affecting the sense.

[12]*Plutarch's Lives*, trans. John Langhorne and William Langhorne . . . . (4 vols. Philadelphia, Hickman & Hazzard, 1822). This was a reprint of the first edition of 1770; the *Life* of Marius is in II, 241-80.

[13]George L. McKay, *American Book Auction Catalogues, 1713–1934* (New York, New York Public Library, 1937), item 642.

[14]McCullough, *op. cit.*, p. 2.

over three hundred volumes. There were also a large number of French plays and books relating to French drama." From his own library, then, he might easily have drawn on earlier English treatments of his subject. One possible source is Thomas Lodge's *The Wounds of Civil War,*[15] but as Professor Mabbott has suggested,[16] this is an uneven imitation of Marlowe's *Tamburlaine,* does not have the scene with Marius brooding in the ruins of Carthage, and places Marius' death off-stage. A more likely background drama is Thomas Otway's *Caius Marius.*[17] This is Romeo and Juliet in Rome rather than Verona, with Marius reminiscent of Montague and Metellus of Capulet. The old soldiers are subordinate to their son and daughter, and the civil disorders of Rome are secondary to the young lovers whose lives follow Shakespeare's play, even to the balcony scene and the double tragedy at the tomb. Marius is led off, a broken and fallen leader nearer to Plutarch's original than Richard Penn Smith's dramatic reading. However, the Otway play could well have suggested the invention of the two lovers in the Smith version. Internal evidence in the manuscript itself makes it clear that Smith was familiar with Ben Jonson's *Catiline;*[18] two speeches of Marius in Act II. Scene 1 are almost verbatim from Jonson. Throughout the play there are echoes, in phrases and arrangement of dialogue, of *Coriolanus, Julius Caesar,* and *Hamlet.* These attributions of sources only suggest the playwright saturated with drama he had read and seen, a writer attracted by a theme not unusual in literature but one particularly adaptable to the moment. Smith's immediate intellectual environment may have had as much to do with his choice of a subject as his recollections of early reading; David Paul Brown, an intimate friend of Smith, produced his own play, *Sertorius,* on December 14, 1830, at the Chestnut Street Theatre, about a month before the presentation of *Caius Marius* at the Arch Street Theatre. A vapid imitation of *Julius Caesar* and Addison's *Cato,* Brown's play is concerned with a young

---

[15] Thomas Lodge, *The Wounds of Civil War, lively set forth in the true Tragedies of Marius and Scilla* (London, Danter, 1594).

[16] Mabbott, *op. cit.,* p. 149.

[17] Thomas Otway, *The history and fall of Caius Marius* (London, for Tho. Flesher, 1680).

[18] Ben Jonson, *The Workes. . . .* (London, Bishop, 1640), pp. 604-05.

soldier who had been under the command of Marius in Gaul but was later banished because of his affiliation with his former leader.[19] This coincidence of parallel inspiration between close friends is not surprising; they were undoubtedly in frequent association. With a contemporary stimulus and earlier dramatic models to influence him, Smith, knowing the audience and the actor for whom he was writing, may well have been directed to his choice by Plutarch's thumbnail sketch for a democratic hero: "[Caius Marius] had neither riches nor eloquence to recommend him; though these were the instruments by which the great men of those times governed the people. His high spirit, however, his indefatigable industry, and plain manner of living, recommended him so effectually to the commonalty, that he gained offices, and by offices, power."[20]

The stages of the composition of the play show Forrest's influence upon it and the growth of the ultimate production. There are two earlier references to the existence of a manuscript prior to 1831. Francis Wemyss, the actor and manager, says in his reminiscences that the play was placed in his hands in 1828, with Southwell considered for the part.[21] He adds, "luckily for the author, it was not produced. Mr. Forrest paid much better for original plays than the managers . . . ." Apart from financial reward, the delay may have been advantageous. Durang says that Henry Southwell "was a native of Dublin, and had all the humorous vivacity of his countrymen . . . a fine-figured young man, with very excellent requisites to sustain juvenile tragic characters, possessing a good deal of spirit and energy. He made a favorable impression in *Romeo* . . . ."[22] Even with aid of make-up and other tools of theatrical illusion, one hardly sees this exuberant Irishman in the role of the moody, aging, and commanding figure of Marius. With the manuscript itself is a note from John Forrester Foot dated 18 May 1829 to Smith, ". . . Have you finished

---

[19]*Plutarch's Lives*, III, 1-24, where the *Life* of Sertorius appears.

[20]*Plutarch's Lives*, II, 244-45.

[21]Francis Courtney Wemyss, *Twenty-six Years of the Life of an Actor and Manager* (New York, Burgess, Stringer, 1847), I, 188.

[22]Charles Durang, *The Philadelphia Stage,* (2nd ser.), III, 242, in the interleaved University of Pennsylvania copy of this collection of articles appearing in the Philadelphia *Sunday Dispatch,* 1854-60.

Marius, upon Kean's Idea? Can I be favour'd with a Perusal of it? Is it true, that, after your having *presented it to him,* he took no notice of you or the Peice [sic]? I wish to do Justice to Literature and Dramatics in general, and therefore I am desirous to have solid Information . . . ."[23] A native Londoner, Foot was on the American stage for some fifteen years after his arrival in 1822, "and though possessing great natural abilities and a fine education, became so reduced in circumstances that he was for a time an inmate of the Almshouse—all his misfortunes being attributable to one unhappy failing."[24] Whatever his bibulous tendencies may have been, he was genuinely interested in the theatre and wrote "A Brief Treatise on the Principles and Advantages of Elocution", (1833). The last two pages of publisher's ads in this 18-page pamphlet announce that "speedily will be Published" an *Essay on the Present State of the Drama.* Bibliographical search indicates that the volume was never published, but one can assume that the proposed work was that referred to in his letter to Smith. The reference to Kean in his letter is even more intriguing. Edmund Kean, the great English Shakespearean actor, had successful tours in America in 1820 to 1821 and 1825 to 1826. The young Forrest modeled his career on Kean and may have introduced him to Smith, although there seems to be no record other than this letter from Foot to establish any relationship. Be that as it may, the existing manuscript is indubitably that prepared for Forrest, in Smith's hand, 199 leaves bound in boards, and containing a wealth of additional material.

The manuscript was purchased at auction by the University of Pennsylvania in 1956, a welcome addition to the existing drama collection, and even more welcome because the author was the grandson of the first Provost. Attempts to establish provenance through the auction house have been unsuccessful. The flyleaf of the manuscript, however, bears the autograph of Horace Wemyss Smith, son of the author, and it must have been in his possession for some time since he initiated the request to Forrest for permission for the revival in 1858. Tipped in with the manu-

[23] University of Pennsylvania manuscript, in Richard Penn Smith Collection.
[24] Joseph N. Ireland, *Records of the New York Stage, 1750–1860* (New York, Morrell, 1866), I, 406-07.

script is a playbill for the second performance [the only located playbill for any of the three Philadelphia presentations in January, 1831]. There are letters from Forrest, William Dunlap, and William B. Wood (those relating to the play are cited in this text); and account sheets between Forrest and Smith. Several newspaper clippings provide reviews hitherto unknown, as well as a playbill and material on the revival, previously unrecorded, in 1858, with Forrest's letter to Horace Wemyss Smith granting permission for the performance as a memorial. There are a number of other clippings and playbills for other appearances by Forrest, particularly his first performance in London at the Drury Lane Theatre, October 17, 1836, when he chose for his English debut *The Gladiator* by his American friend, Robert Montgomery Bird.

Edwin Forrest, the star in *Caius Marius* and, more importantly, the immediate motivation for the play itself, was only twenty-five when he first presented Smith's verse tragedy. He was already on his way toward a reputation as the first great American actor. Born in Philadelphia in 1806, he made his debut at the Walnut Street Theatre at the age of fourteen in the usual part for the fledgling actor, Young Norval in John Home's *Douglas.* For the next six years, until his successful opening in New York as Othello at the Park Theatre, Forrest traveled the frontier circuits of Pittsburgh and the Ohio River towns, to New Orleans, then up to Albany in 1825 where he met and played with Edmund Kean, in America on his second tour. The encouragement and example of the great English actor helped to set the tone of Forrest's vigorous and electrifying style. While he excelled in Shakespearean tragedies until the end of his career, his strong sense of national feeling prompted his desire for recognition for American actors and playwrights. By 1828, Forrest's professional and financial security was such as to prompt him to offer prizes for plays by native authors. To his friend, William Leggett, poet, journalist, and later assistant editor, under William Cullen Bryant, of the New York *Evening Post,* he sent the following request: "Dear Sir, Feeling extremely desirous that dramatic letters should be more cultivated in my native country, and believing that the dearth of writers in that department is rather the result of a want of the proper incentive than of any deficiency of the requisite

Edwin Forrest

talents, I should feel greatly obliged to you if you would com-
municate to the public, in the next number of the 'Critic,' the
following offer. To the author of the best Tragedy, in five acts,
of which the hero or principal character shall be an aboriginal
of this country, the sum of five hundred dollars, and half of the
proceeds of the third representation, with my own gratuitous
services on that occasion. The award to be made by a committee
of literary and theatrical gentlemen."[25]

One of Forrest's biographers believed that these prizes, some-
times apparently twice the initial offer, encouraged the writing
of some two hundred plays, most of them mercifully now in
oblivion.[26] The nine which survived, to be known as the Forrest
Prize Plays, were as follows, with their dates of production:
Metamora: or, The Last of the Wampanoags, by John Augustus
Stone, December 15, 1829; *Caius Marius,* by Richard Penn Smith,
January 12, 1831; *Pelopidas: or, The Fall of the Polemarchs,* by
Robert Montgomery Bird, accepted but not produced by Forrest;
The Gladiator, by Bird, September 26, 1831; *Oralloossa,* by
Bird, October 10, 1832; *The Ancient Briton,* by Stone, March
27, 1833; *The Broker of Bogota,* by Bird, February 12, 1834;
Jack Cade, by Robert T. Conrad, first produced as *Aylmere* by
another actor, later by Forrest under its final title, May 24, 1841;
Mohammed, The Arabian Prophet, by G. H. Miles, October 27,
1851, but not produced by Forrest. It is interesting to note that
of these nine dramatic survivors, only two, Stone's *Metamora* and
Bird's *Oralloossa,* fulfilled the requirement that the chief character should be an aboriginal American. However, Forrest's first
motivation was, reasonably, to find a vehicle for his talents and
a play that would appeal to his audiences in an age that preferred the direct histrionics of forceful action to the subtleties
of psychological introspection.

There can be no doubt of the impetus which Forrest gave to
the American playwright by his financial encouragement. As
Wemyss pointed out, Forrest paid much better for original plays
than the American managers would offer, since they could obtain the best English plays for the price of a few printed copies,
in a time when there was no dramatic copyright, and they were

[25] As quoted in Montrose J. Moses, *The American Dramatist* (Boston, Little,
Brown, 1925), p. 120.
[26] William R. Alger, *Life of Edwin Forrest* (Philadelphia, Lippincott, 1877), I, 169.

not likely, therefore, "to risk hundreds on native productions, which, unaided by the talent of an acknowledged star, seldom outlive the first night of representation."[27] The prize of five hundred dollars, or, as it often turned out to be, a thousand, was a munificent sum in the 1830's. It must be remembered that Forrest's contribution of his free services for the third performance of one of the plays was tantamount to another one hundred dollars, and his prestige could generally be counted on to produce a full house, with the author receiving half the proceeds, averaging as much as another hundred. Later dramatic historians have criticized Forrest for his "selfishness" in retaining these plays for his exclusive use and, in many cases, not permitting their publication. However, his own age viewed the matter in quite a different light. There was no contemporary criticism of his possessive attitude toward a product which he had purchased for a high price; property was *property,* and the author resigned his right to his play when Forrest or any other actor or manager bought it.

The financial stimulus for native playwrights was vastly important, but it was Forrest's insistence on the actual production of these American plays that had the most lasting effect. When he made his first appearance on an English stage, in 1836, he chose a play with a classical theme, with a hero whose tragic dignity was in the long tradition from Euripides to Shakespeare. However, Robert Montgomery Bird's *The Gladiator* was a stirring parade of democratic virtues, with Forrest figuratively waving the American flag. His spectacular performance, and others which followed in England and America, was not forgotten by his audience. A laudatory comment, with a subtle qualification, twelve years later, illustrated the effect of his influence: "He has created a school in his art, strictly American, and he stands forth as the very embodiment, as it were, of the masses of American character. Hence his peculiarities. Hence his amazing success. And further, Mr. Forrest in his acting is not merely the embodiment of a national character, but he is the beau ideal of a peculiar phase of that character—its democratic idiosyncrasy. Of this

---

[27]Wemyss, *Twenty-six Years of the Life of an Actor and Manager,* I, 188.

both physically and in his artistical execution, he is a complete living illustration."[28]

Forrest may have been the personification of the robust exuberance of the uninhibited American, but the American theatre of his time, particularly the season of 1830-31 when *Caius Marius* was produced, was in a comparable state of experimentation, change, and development. The venerable Chestnut Street Theatre in Philadelphia, built in 1791 and elegantly patterned after the Theatre Royal at Bath, had passed the period of its dominance under the management of Wood and Warren. The Walnut Street Theatre, built as a circus in 1809 and used as a theatre since 1811, had been sumptuously redesigned by John Haviland in 1828, but was operating at a loss in competition with the Arch Street Theatre. The scene of the performance of *Caius Marius* and many other native American plays, the Arch had been built in 1828, designed in the classic revival style by William Strickland, but even the aggressive management of Thomas Archer, Robert Maywood, William Walton, and shortly William Forrest, brother of Edwin, could not keep up the pace in the fierce competition for audiences. Average prices were $1.00 for box seats, $0.75 for the pit and $0.25 for the gallery, but in 1828, the Walnut, in a battle with the Chestnut, dropped to $0.50, $0.37½, and $0.25 for the same seats. The opening of the new theatre on the north side of Arch Street, west of 6th Street, only increased the rivalry.

Durang and other contemporary observers of theatrical history were aware of changing times. They complained of the fickle audiences and their preferences for the "follies of fashion," resulting from "mawkish morality, notions and speculations of politicians—all that farrago of chimerical ideas and false position," and concluded flatly that the taste of the public had radically altered.[29] There was general consensus that the star system, in opposition to the established repertoire companies, was financially ruinous and only fed the popular fancy for the spectacular performer or the bizarre extravaganza. What they were witnessing was, of course, the democratization of the theatrical audiences. Nevertheless, the demands of the successful performer were in-

[28] Quoted from *Albion* (New York), Sept. 2, 1848, in Barnard Hewitt, *Theatre U.S.A. 1665 to 1957* (New York, McGraw-Hill, 1959), p. 109.

[29] Durang, (3rd ser.), III, 14.

deed threatening the survival of the standard theatrical system and were directly contributory to the collapse of numerous theatres. Popular stars such as Wallack and Forrest were demanding as much as $200 a night—which they seldom received because the house frequently did no better than $150. Durang correctly laid the poor attendance to an economic decline, a period of high prices and sluggish trade; he drew a melancholy picture of the condition of the supporting actors, "with nothing to console our distresses and to relieve our persons from imprisonment, but the benefit of the Insolvent Act. With the most scanty credit and sympathy, half-starved, we still tried to look cheerful and to entertain the public even to laughter. During the after season, which reached to the 30th of July, a portion positively lived in the dressing-rooms of the theatre; and thus playing as they could, got up entertainments with a crippled company. . ."[30]

To add to the unhappy financial situation, the winter of 1830-1831 was excessively cold, with a succession of heavy snowstorms that kept the public at home. In the week of the performance of *Caius Marius,* Durang reported that January 20 was the coldest day of the winter, with severe snowstorms. He said that the unheated theatres were ice houses, that "nothing short of a crammed house had any effect on modifying an icy temperature," that the sparse audience sat silent, muffled in wraps, loath to applaud, but instead they beat tattoos with their feet in an attempt to stir up sluggish circulation, and he concluded that it was indeed a dreary, dull winter.[31]

In desperation, the managers tried every device to attract an audience. Durang sourly reported that "a steam carriage, which whirled four persons in its body around the ball room of the Masonic Hall, in Chestnut Street, excited much attention, doing a better business than the theatres."[32] Every possible inducement was tried, even to "Jocko," or the "Brazilian Ape," of whom Durang could note, "[The actor] played the ape naturally enough, exhibiting great agility in his various gyrations and antics. In Jocko's death scene he threw out tragic expressions of the Kean force and style which quite electrified the audience."[33] The ap-

[30]*Ibid.,* (3rd ser.), III, p. 20.
[31]*Ibid.,* (3rd ser.), III, pp. 15-16.
[32]*Ibid.,* p. 30.
[33]*Ibid.,* p. 14.

pearance of Master Burke, the twelve-year old prodigy, was a
financial blessing to the Arch Street Theatre in December; he
was enthusiastically received as Dr. Pangloss, Richard III, and
Sir Abel Handy in *Speed the Plow*. Durang could only comment,
"Do, good reader, imagine this childish abortion of character beside a Warren, a Kilner, a Dowton, etc."[34] The height of desperate invention was the battle between the Chestnut and the Arch
for Mlle. D'Jick, the elephant of Siam, which had been enthusiastically received in New York. The Arch Street manager got to
New York after Lamb from the Chestnut thought he had secured
the act but had failed to sign the contract. Both theatres an-
nounced the elephant, but the Arch won out only after the
court made a legal decision of such last-second character that
most of the audience had left.[35]

All of these troubles and diversions were indicative of a perilous
theatrical condition; however, an analysis of the season at the
three houses shows an astonishing activity in comparison with
the modern stage.[36] The length of the season varied according
to public response, and it is to be remembered that a play would
generally have a run of three nights, with a renewal later in the
season if the presentation had been originally successful.

The Chestnut opened October 18, 1830, closing the winter
season April 9, 1831. In that period were presented 56 comedies,
13 operas, 1 ballet, 22 historical plays, 13 tragedies, and 8 melodramas. Among the comedies were *The School for Scandal, She
Stoops to Conquer,* and Shakespeare's *As You Like It, Twelfth
Night,* and *Comedy of Errors.* The operas included *Inkle and
Yarico,* and a comic version of *Home, Sweet Home.* Popular
historical productions were *Virginius, Metamora, Sertorius, Pizarro, Richard II,* and *Richard III. Macbeth* and *Hamlet* were the
preferred tragedies.

The season at the Walnut was not a good one; the theatre
opened August 30, 1830, and closed December 18. It presented
10 comedies, 5 operas, 2 historical plays, 1 tragedy, and 17 melo-
dramatic productions. Successful comedies were *The Heir at
Law* and *Merchant of Venice.* The operas included *Barber of*

[34]*Ibid.,* p. 31.

[35]*Ibid.,* pp. 15-17.

[36]This analysis is drawn from Durang (3rd ser.), Vol. III, Season of 1830-31.
Farces and after-pieces are not included.

Seville and *Paul and Virginia. Pizarro* was a favorite historical piece, and *King Lear* was the most popular tragedy. Of the melodramas, *The Bombardment of Algiers* was the most successful, with 11 performances. Others were *Will Watch, the Bold Smuggler, The Floating Beacon,* and *The Night Hag; or, St. Swithin's Chair.*

The Arch Street Theatre opened August 30, 1830; Archer and Maywood closed the theatre late in February, moved the company to Baltimore, and reopened in Philadelphia on April 18, 1831, closing the season early in May. There were 24 comedies offered, 9 operas, 19 historical plays, 19 melodramas, and 16 tragedies. The comedies included *The Rivals* and *Merchant of Venice.* The operas were *Guy Mannering, Marriage of Figaro, The Barber of Seville,* and *The Tempest,* altered by Garrick into a musical production. Among the historical plays were *Richard III, Pizarro,* and *Metamora.* The most popular melodrama was *Valmondi, or the Tomb of Terrors,* with a number of dramatizations of Scott's novels. The tragedies included *Othello, Hamlet, Julius Caesar,* and *Caius Marius.*

It is immediately evident that in serious drama Shakespeare still dominated the American stage, with later seventeenth-and-eighteenth-century English dramatists given their proper due. The historical plays, exclusive of Shakespeare, were tending more toward a recognition of the current scene: the Barbary pirates came in for their share of attention, and Durang reports that "The Marseilles" was sung in every public and private gathering throughout the city to celebrate and commend the French Revolution of 1830.[37] The American drama was evidently coming into its own; Richard Penn Smith and Edwin Forrest made their contribution to this season when they produced *Caius Marius.*

It is difficult to determine how long Forrest had been contemplating the production of the play; however, from the following two letters to Smith, it is evident that there was some consideration of a performance as early as the autumn of 1830.

Dear Smith—
   I rec'd by the hands of Mr. Walker what you sent of the MSS. I like it much, together with your intended alterations but still loathe to lose the points 'his capture and attempted assassination,' yet they *must* give way

[37]Durang, *op. cit.,* III, 30.

to the *general* good. I want an appropriate speech for the conclusion of
the 2'd Act, say five or six lines making *Sulpitius* to exit after Mar—I will
but get my sword and then attend you

Exit Sulpitius

Here then I desire the speech so that Marius may end the act *alone*—
Be sure and send on the remainder according to promise without fail. I have
not made up my mind whether to bring it out in Boston or N.Y. I will,
however, produce it.as soon as possible.

Yours sincerely,
Edwin Forrest[38]

Two weeks later Forrest wrote at more length from New York.

Dear Smith   [New York, October 7, 1830]

I have rec'd the 4th and 5th Acts of Marius but as yet have not perused
them *attentively.* The 3'd Act is yet wanting to complete the play—could
you send it on so as to reach here by 12 o'clock on Sat. next it would be
well as on the afternoon of that day I shall depart for Boston however it
makes no material difference for by sending it addressed to me at the
Park Theatre it would be forwarded with care to Boston. I have increasing
pride for the Tragedy it is destined to make a great hit. We must take our
time however to produce it giving all the proper preliminaries such as
Rehearsal, Costume, and the newspaper mention by implication tho' of
the latter if it was not the *fashion* there would in my mind be no necessity;
its own merit can stand the hazard of the die, but of eulogy there must
be the 'due infusion' before I leave town I will leave the necessary instructions . . . .

I will have the parts of Marius copied for Boston, N. York & Philada.

Yours sincerely,
Edwin Forrest[39]

However much Forrest may have deprecated advance publicity,
he saw to it that mention was made in Philadelphia and New
York papers. Two unidentified clippings with the manuscript announce the forthcoming production in Philadelphia, with the
writer stating that he has seen the manuscript and is "happy in
testifying as to the striking beauty and force of many of its
passages." This may well have appeared in the New York *Mer-
cantile Advertiser,* whose editor, James Lawson, was a close friend
of Forrest from the time he had enthusiastically reviewed the
actor's first appearance in New York in 1826. Lawson wrote to

[38]Autographed letter [New York, September 25 (1830?)]. Smith followed
Forrest's instructions regarding the change to be made. *Cf.* Act II, Scene 3, p. 23 of
following text. Letter at University of Pennsylvania.

[39]Autographed letter, Richard Penn Smith Collection, University of Pennsylvania.

Dear Smith

I rec.d by the hands of Mr. Walker what you sent of the MSS. I like it much, together with your intended alterations but still loathe to lose the points "his capture and attempted assassination" yet they must give way for the general good. I want an appropriate speech for the conclusion of the 2.d Act say five or six lines making Sulpitius to exit after

Mar— I will but get my sword and then attend you

Here then I desire the speech or that Marius may   Exit Sulp-
end the act alone —

Be sure and send on the remainder according to promise without fail. I have not made up my mind whether to bring it out in Boston or N.Y. I will however produce it as soon as possible

yours sincerely

Smith from New York, December 26, 1830, ". . . Your Tragedy
I learn, is to be produced in Phila on 12 Jany — I wish you all
manner of success. It is the intention of Wetmore and myself to
be present at its first representation, God, and business willing—
when I shall be glad to claim you, not only as a correspondent,
but also as a personal acquaintance. We have several packets
below—the news of them will crowd our columns tomorrow, but
on Thursday morning an article in it about Caius Marius shall
appear . . . ."[40]

There is no record of Lawson's presence, but many others of
Forrest's and Smith's friends were in the Arch Street Theatre to
see the latest production. The concensus was generally that the
play itself had merit, but the actors, with the exception of
Forrest, did not do credit to their parts. The "proper preliminaries
such as Rehearsal" which Forrest had urged seem not to have been
carried out. Most of the contemporary writers felt that the play
had been mismanaged,[41] and Durang's comments may serve as
an illustration for them all. "The play was dramatically con-
structed, with vigor of language and harmony of versification,
eventuating in poetical justice. It was written with a view to the
development of Mr. Forrest's peculiar powers, which were well
fitted to impart to the subject all its terrific historical colorings.
It did not receive that study and attention from the corps engaged
in it that it merited. Forrest, as *Caius Marius,* acquitted himself
admirably; and Mrs. Sharpe, as well as the calibre of her role admitted 'did that she did' with credit. The rest were 'leather and
prunella.'[42] The performers were shamefully imperfect . . . ."[43]
A more laudatory review in the *Daily Chronicle* reported that
the play was produced to "a very numerous and respectable audience," that the plan of the tragedy "is well conceived—the plot

[40] Autographed letter, in University of Pennsylvania Library.

[41] *Cf.* Wemyss, *Twenty-six Years of the Life of an Actor and Manager,* I, 118;
James Rees, *The Life of Edwin Forrest* (Philadelphia, Peterson, 1847), pp. 414-15;
William B. Wood, *Personal Recollections of the Stage* (Philadelphia, Baird, 1855), p.
363.

[42] Here, "a matter of indifference"; a misinterpretation of a quotation from Pope's
Essay on Man: "Worth makes the man and want of it, the fellow. The rest is all but
leather and prunella." The context refers to the difference in rank between the
cobbler's apron of leather and the parson's garb, made from a material named
"prunella."

[43] Durang, *op. cit,* (3rd ser.), III, 32.

properly developed—the characters judiciously designed and sustained, and the dialogue is remarkable for vigour and beauty. Several of the scenes were highly effective; and, altogether, we think the piece decidedly superior to any native tragedy which has been brought upon the American stage."[44]

David Paul Brown, Philadelphia lawyer and Smith's good friend, wrote the prologue for the play and no doubt was present for the performance. Brown's *Sertorius,* which dealt with an historical figure in the Marius story, had been produced at the Chestnut on December 14, 1830, before a brilliant audience.[45]

Caius Marius was produced on January 12, again on the 14th, with the author's benefit on Monday, the 17th. A detailed accounting of receipts for that last performance, included with the manuscript, reveal that the total amount received was $214.25, with half of that amount going to the author, out of which he paid Mrs. Sharpe, the leading lady, $10.70, leaving Smith a disappointing total of only $96.42. This was poor return indeed, but Smith, like David Paul Brown, took a philosophical view of the situation, and was by no means discouraged from further dramatic endeavor. He had a detached attitude toward his literary productions, especially the plays, recognizing that the success of a dramatic production may be dependent on unpredictable circumstances—the weather, the personality of the star, and the cast of the audience as well as that of the play.

Four years after Richard Penn Smith died in 1854 at the age of fifty-five at the family home at the Falls of the Schuylkill, James Rees, dramatic historian and one of the biographers of Forrest, wrote to Horace Wemyss Smith, the dramatist's son, suggesting a revival of the play. In a clipping preserved with the manuscript, Rees says that his request was "for the purpose of fanning the embers of a national dramatic flame, that at one time burnt brightly on the altar of Thespis, but which is now flickering in the ashes of its own dead fruit." Horace W. Smith approached Forrest, who replied, "Dear Sir, Your note of yesterday asking permission to have the play of Caius Marius, which was written by your father expressly for me reproduced at the Walnut St. Theatre; I have great pleasure in assenting to your re-

[44]Philadelphia *Daily Chronicle,* January 17, 1831.
[45]Durang, *op. cit,* (3rd ser.), III, 11-12.

quest, and am confident that with the combined talent and skill of the Walnut St. company, the play will be creditably and ably performed."[46]

The play was produced November 8 and 9, 1858, at the Walnut Street Theatre, then under the capable management of Mrs. D. P. Bowers, who took one of the supporting roles, with F. B. Conway playing Marius. The cast is given in the pages prefatory to the text of the play. From a clipping preserved with the manuscript, it is evident that the performances were well attended by a fashionable audience. The review continues:

> In the construction of this tragedy, Mr. Smith did not overlook dramatic effect. Its literary character is such as to have elicited praise from the best critics in the country .... In justice to Mrs. Bowers, who manifested a laudable disposition to revive the production of one of our ablest dramatists, we must say, that every attention was paid to the getting "Caius Marius" up properly ....

Forrest occupied one of the conspicuous boxes, and the reviewer commented, "Mr. Conway's impersonation of *Marius* was remarkably fine, and when it is remembered that the eyes of one of the most distinguished tragedians of the day were looking down on him from a private box, and for whom the piece was originally written, his presence of mind must have been strongly tested."

Rees's orotund reference to the "embers of a national dramatic flame" may have been exaggerated, but certainly the audiences of 1831 saw the play in the light of a national expression of exuberant identification. *Caius Marius* and the other Forrest Prize Plays were indicative of a creative effort to provide original drama attractive to an American audience that was receptive to performances appealing to a strong nationalistic and democratic sensibility. Eight of the nine plays provide a capsule commentary on the changing taste in the American theatre. While only Stone's *Metamora* had its locale in the United States, and Bird's *The Gladiator* and *Pelopidas,* Stone's *The Ancient Briton,* and *Caius Marius* are based on ancient history, the democratic theme was consistently present: the value was the struggle of the individual against a corrupt or aristocratic establishment, winning his way by the exercise of a spirit of patriotism that identified the common man and his peers as the true patricians of the human race.

[46]Autographed letter, Philadelphia, Sept. 8, 1858, University of Pennsylvania Library.

Philadelphia
September 8. 1858

Dear Sir,

Your note of yesterday
asking permission to have the
play of Caius Marius, which was
written by your father expressly
for me, reproduced at the
Walnut St theatre; I have great
pleasure in assenting to your
request, and am confident that
with the combined talent and
skill of the Walnut St company,
the play will be creditably and
ably performed.

Truly yours
Edwin Forrest.

H. W. Smith Esq

Note on the Text

The manuscript consists of 200 leaves, 23cm. x 20cm., bound in brown quarter-leather over paper-covered boards. The text, in blank verse, is written in ink on the recto of the leaves, with stage directions and alterations in text occasionally on the facing verso, as indicated in the footnotes. When the notes refer to "facing page," it is understood that the reference is to the manuscript, not to the present text. The manuscript is obviously an acting copy in which the continuity from speech to speech of the five-stress line has not been observed by the convention of moving the remnants toward the right-hand margin. For clarity, we have restored the conventional manner of setting dramatic verse.

This manuscript was used for the Philadelphia performance in 1831 and for the revival in 1858. The cuts of speeches or scenes in the play could have been made for any one of these performances, and it is obviously impossible to know who made the deletions. The cuts are in either pen or pencil, and are so described in the notes.

Lines of the text are numbered consecutively within a scene.

The author's spelling is nearly impeccable; the punctuation is more erratic, the most common omissions being commas and apostrophes. These omissions have not been corrected. In the footnotes, cancellations, additions and alterations indicated in the text are by Smith unless another hand is so described. The author's spellings, following the Langhorne translation of Plutarch, have been retained for proper names: *Caius* for *Gaius,* *Sylla* for *Sulla,* and *Sulpitius* for *Sulpicius.*

Canceled readings and stage directions are not closed by punctuation unless the punctuation is part of the passage.

Stage directions are printed as the author showed them in this unedited Ms. but are not included in the line count.

Stage directions in other hands are in italics in the footnotes where directly quoted; stage directions that required editorial reconstruction are in the footnotes, within brackets.

PHILADELPHIA
THEATRE,
ARCH STREET.

Second Night of Caius Marius.

The New Tragedy of CAIUS MARIUS having been received by a brilliant and overflowing house, with deep attention, aud bursts of enthusiastic applause, will be repeated this Evening.

SECOND NIGHT OF THE ENGAGEMENT OF
Mrs. SHARPE;
AND
Mr. E. FORREST.

Friday Evening, Jan. 14, 1831

WILL BE PRESENTED WITH NEW SCENERY, DRESSES, DECORATIONS, PROPERTIES, &c.

THE NEW TRAGEDY,
Written by Richard Penn Smith, Esq.

OF

CAIUS MARIUS.

A PROLOGUE,
Written by David Paul Brown, Esq.
WILL BE SPOKEN BY MR. ARCHER.

Caius Marius, - **Mr. E. Forrest.**

Metellus, - - Mr Archer.	Cinna, - - - Mr. Walton.
Sylla, - - - Mr. Maywood.	Granius, - - - Mr. Smith.
Sulpitius, - - Mr. Rowbotham.	1st Centurion, - - Mr. Broad:
Antonius' - - Mr. Porter.	2d do. - - - Mr. Jones.

Citizens, Soldiers, &c. &c-

Martha, - **Mrs. Sharpe.**

Metella, - - Mrs, Rowbotham. | Servia, - - Miss. Coleman.

IN ACT FIRST:—

Marius's Triumphal Entry into Rome,
GRAND PROCESSION.

TO CONCLUDE WITH THE LAUGHABLE FARCE OF THE

Sleeping Draught.

Doctor Vincolo, - Mr. Watson.	Gabrioto, - - Mr. J. Fisher.
Farmer Bruno, - Mr. Jones.	Yaldo, - - - Mr. Porter.
Rinaldo, - - Mr. Smith,	1st Man, - - Mr Broad,
Popolino, - - Mr.W. Chapman	2d do. - - - Mr. Derr'
Francisca, - - Miss Coleman,	Nonna, - - Mrs. Rowbotham.

Cast of the 1831 Philadelphia
Performance of *Caius Marius*[1]

EDWIN FORREST. *Caius Marius.* The only American-born member of the cast, with the possible exception of one of the minor characters, Forrest was born in Philadelphia, March 9, 1806. His first theatrical appearance was at the age of fourteen as Norval in James Home's *Douglas,* at the Walnut Street Theatre in 1820. Six years later, in his first New York appearance as Othello, he achieved stardom overnight. *Caius Marius* was thus relatively early in a dramatic career that lasted almost until his death in 1872.

THOMAS ARCHER. *Metellus.* Born in England in 1789, he made his first American appearance in New York at the Bowery Theatre in 1829 as Richard III. At the time of the presentation of *Caius Marius,* he was one of the managers of the Arch Street Theatre with Maywood and Walton. He later returned to England and died there in 1848.

ROBERT C. MAYWOOD. *Sylla.* Born in Scotland, he also made his first American appearance as Richard III, at the Park Theatre in 1819. He became the manager of the Chestnut Street Theatre as one of the firm of Maywood and Company, 1832 to 1840. He later traveled in Ohio and "elsewhere," Wemyss remarked, as he lost Maywood's trail.

H. H. ROWBOTHAM. *Sulpitius.* English-born, he made his first American appearance at the Chestnut Street Theatre in 1828 as Dumont in *Jane Shore.* He was joint lessee and stage manager as a member of the firm of Maywood and Company. He died in Philadelphia in 1837.

---

[1] The source for these biographical data, unless otherwise indicated, is Frances Courtney Wemyss, *Wemyss' Chronology of the American Stage from 1752 to 1852* (New York, [c.1852]), an alphabetical arrangement with appendix.

WILLIAM WALTON. *Cinna.* Born in England, he made his American debut at the Federal Street Theatre in Boston in 1827. He was the manager of the Arch Street Theatre in 1830, later the manager of the Museum in Baltimore. He returned to England and was for a time the stage manager of the Princesses' Theatre in London. He died in the 1840's.

Identification of the remaining men in the cast must be conjectural. PORTER. *Antonius.* He was possibly Charles Porter, born in New Jersey, and first appeared at the South Street Theatre in Philadelphia in 1817. He was manager of theatres in Pittsburgh and Vicksburg in 1847. SMITH. *Granius.* He was probably William Henry Sedley who unofficially used the surname of Smith. A native Welshman, he made his first American appearance at the Walnut Street Theatre in 1827. He later appeared in New York and was for a time the manager of Kimball's Museum in Boston. BROAD. *1st Centurion.* He must remain unidentified for the present. JONES. *2nd Centurion.* He was probably William Jones who, with William Duffy and William Forrest, brother of Edwin, was manager of the Arch Street Theatre for a time in the 1830's.

MRS. SHARPE. *Martha.* Neither Durang nor Wemyss supply information as to her origin, Wemyss giving only the information that she was "an excellent general actress, long attached to the Park Theatre, New York, married Captain Brevoort, of the United States Marine Corps, and retired from the profession." Her last appearance on the New York stage was at the National Theatre, as Lady Macbeth, November 8, 1839.[2]

MRS. ROWBOTHAM. *Metella.* Born in London, she made her first appearance in America at the Chestnut Street Theatre in 1828. Durang[3] adds that she "was originally a dancer, or a *coryphée,* at the Italian Opera House, London." After the death of Rowbotham, she married Robert Hamilton and died in Philadelphia in 1839.

MISS COLEMAN. *Servia.* Durang[4] supplies the information that Jane Coleman, born in England, "was very useful and respectable in all parts, but her talent did not aspire to the exalted of tragedy

[2] Odell, *Annals of the New York Stage* (New York, 1928), IV, 338.
[3] Durang (2nd ser.), III, 253.
[4] Durang (3rd ser.), III, 26.

or comedy. Her fate we do not know. She appeared for the first time on any stage at the Arch street house . . . in 1829. She remained some few seasons after among our theatres in Baltimore and here."

This, Monday Evening, Nov 8th, 1858,

Will be Revived, by permission of

EDWIN FORREST, ESQ.

For whom it was written, by the late RICHARD PENN SMITH, Esq.,

THE CELEBRATED TRAGEDY,

IN FIVE ACTS, ENTITLED

CAIUS

MARIUS!

☞ LOOK AT THE CAST! ☜

Caius Marius,	-	-	Mr F. B. Conway	1st Citizen,	-	Mr Hemple
Metellus,	-	-	Mr Richings	2d Citizen,	-	Mr Williams
Sylla,	-	-	Mr McDonough	3d Citizen,	-	Mr Porter
Sulpitius,	-	-	Mr H. A. Perry	4th Citizen,	-	Mr Poole
Antonius,	-	-	Mr Young	5th Citizen,	-	Mr J. Reed
Cinna,	-	-	Mr Dubois	6th Citizen,	-	Mr Mathews
Granius,	-	-	Mr E. F. Keach	Martha,	-	Mrs F. B. Conway
Centurion,	-	-	Mr Crocker	Metella,	-	Mrs D. P. Bowers
Cimbrian,	-	-	Mr Greene	Servia,	-	Mrs H. A. Perry

This, Tuseday Evening, Nov. 9th, 1858,

SECOND NIGHT, BY PERMISSION OF

EDWIN FORREST, ESQ.

For whom it was written by the late

RICHARD PENN SMITH, Esq.,

The Celebrated Tragedy, in 5 Acts, entitled

CAIUS

MARIUS!

☞ LOOK AT THE CAST! ☜

Caius Marius,	-	-	Mr F. B. Conway	1st Citizen,	-	Mr Hemple
Metellus,	-	-	Mr Richings	2d Citizen,	-	Mr Williams
Sylla,	-	-	Mr McDonough	3d Citizen,	-	Mr Porter
Sulpitius,	-	-	Mr H. A. Perry	4th Citizen,	-	Mr Poole
Antonius,	-	-	Mr Young	5th Citizen,	-	Mr J. Reed
Cinna,	-	-	Mr Dubois	6th Citizen,	-	Mr Mathews
Granius,	-	-	Mr E. F. Keach	Martha,	-	Mrs F. B. Conway
Centurion,	-	-	Mr Crocker	Metella,	-	Mrs D. P. Bowers
Cimbrian,	-	-	Mr Greene	Servia,	-	Mrs. H. A. Perry

Cast of the 1858 Philadelphia
Performances of *Caius Marius*

The principal actors of the memorial revival were:

FREDERICK BARTLETT CONWAY. *Caius Marius.* The son of the tragedian, W. H. Conway, he was born near Bristol, England, February 10, 1819. He had theatrical experience in the provinces and in London before becoming the leading man of the Broadway Theatre, New York, in 1850. In May 1852, he married Miss Sarah Crocker, the sister of Mrs. D. P. Bowers. They were at the Arch Street and Walnut Street Theatres in Philadelphia in the 1850's and toured throughout the country, performing particularly at Pike's Opera House in Cincinnati. They were at Sadler's Wells in London in 1861. Returning to New York, they held the lease on the Park Theatre from 1864 until 1874, when Conway died at the age of fifty-six. He frequently appeared with Forrest in supporting roles. "Mr. Forrest has on more than one occasion drawn the attention of the public to Mr. Conway's merits, by leading him before the curtain to share with him their plaudits."[1]

PETER RICHINGS. *Metellus.* Born in London in 1797, he held an army commission for a brief time, studied for the law, but became permanently infatuated with the stage. To avoid family interference, he came to America and made his debut at the Park Theatre in New York in 1821. After an indifferent reception, he applied himself to learning the profession so successfully that he was at the Park for thirteen seasons. He went to Philadelphia in 1840, had various theatrical associations there and in Baltimore, retiring from the stage in 1863. He died at his home in Media, Pennsylvania, in 1871.[2]

---

[1] New York *Spirit of the Times,* Oct. 6, 1855.
[2] *The New York Clipper,* Nov. 5, 1911.

JOHN MC DONOUGH. *Sylla.* Born in London in 1825, at the age of four he was brought to Philadelphia by his parents. After some education, he learned the trades of baker and leather-dresser. The attraction of the stage was irresistible; after a disastrous debut in Boston about 1846, he learned his profession in touring companies in Canada, Baltimore, and Pittsburgh. He began a ten-year association with Philadelphia theatres in 1848. He was a member of the Walnut Street stock company from 1852, playing occasionally with Edwin Forrest. After 1858, he went frequently on tour to the West Coast, New Orleans, New York, and Australia. He was indefatigable in his search for talent, making more than one trip to Europe to find suitable attractions. After a long and varied career, he made his last appearance at Low's Opera House in Providence, Rhode Island on October 8, 1881, and died in his home in Philadelphia on February 15, 1882.[3]

H. A. PERRY. *Sulpitius.* A native Philadelphian, he was born December 25, 1826. As a boy, he did stable work and rode in horse races and later learned the tailoring trade. However, the theatre became increasingly attractive. He made his debut, when about nineteen, at the Walnut Street Theatre in Philadelphia as Malcolm in *Macbeth.* In 1851, he was leading man at the Broadway in New York. Until 1859, when he was again at the Walnut, he toured and starred in the West and in Canada. His last engagements in the East were at Niblo's Garden, New York. In 1860 Perry went to San Francisco, where he concluded his theatrical career, dying there on January 22, 1862. His obituary predicted no enduring fame for him, but suggested some of the qualities which no doubt made him a convincing Sulpitius, boisterous and aggressive. "Mr. Perry apparently thought that he was destined to shine most in tragedy and high comedy, but the public verdict was against his pretensions in that way. His strength lay in eccentric or low comedy, and there he showed great force of acting and much genuine humor . . . . His voice was too harsh and unmodulated, his gestures were too ungraceful, and his limbs too bulky and unwieldy, to suit the polished nature of the heroic or the courtly of the higher drama. But in his proper range of characters, Mr. Perry was a great acquisition to our local stage,

[3] *The New York Clipper,* Sept. 2, 1911.

and his place cannot very well be supplied by any actor at present among us.

"He was a popular favorite, and that circumstance prevented public indignation, on many occasions, from falling on him on account of some personal irregularities. Let us bestow a kind thought on him who has so often ministered to our delight, and forget his faults. Peace to his memory."[4]

SAMMUEL CONIERS DU BOIS. *Cinna.* "Sammuel Coniers Du Bois died on Jan. 17, 1898, at Philadelphia, Pa., where he was born in 1834. From occupying a position as callboy in the old Walnut Street Theatre, he rose until, in the early fifties, he became manager of the Pittsburgh Theatre. He returned to Philadelphia to act in Mrs. Garrison's Stock Company at the Walnut, retiring temporarily in 1870. He reappeared at various times with Edwin Booth, John McCullough, and Frederick Warde, and managed, during the season of 1891–92, the Richmond, Va., Academy of Music. Mr. Du Bois was a man of scholarly attainments, of wide culture, and of unusual executive powers. As historian, as business man, as manager and as actor he was highly esteemed in his native city and elsewhere."[5]

MRS. F. B. CONWAY. *Martha.* A sister of Mrs. D. P. Bowers, and the daughter of a clergyman, Sarah Crocker was born in Litchfield, Connecticut, in 1834. She reached theatrical prominence at Wallack's Theatre in New York in 1854, two years after her marriage to Conway. They traveled as stars to Philadelphia and the West. She successfully managed, with her husband's assistance, the Park and Brooklyn Theatres in the decade following the close of the Civil War, starring there and across the country with her daughters, Minnie and Lillian. She died suddenly in New York in April, 1875.[6]

MRS. D. P. BOWERS. *Metella.* ". . . Miss Crocker, since Mrs. D. P. Bowers, made her first appearance on the stage as Amanthis, in 'The Child of Nature' [Dec. 3, 1845, Park Theatre, New York] . . . . Miss Crocker was a native of Connecticut, and possessed a reasonable share of Yankee energy, enterprise and spirit. She be-

---

[4] San Francisco *Bulletin,* Jan. 22, 1862.
[5] Obituary appearing in *The New York Dramatic Mirror,* Jan. 29, 1898.
[6] New York *Spirit of the Times,* May 8, 1875.

came Mrs. Bowers in the summer of 1848, and after her husband's death, which occurred in 1857, took the management of one of the theatres in Philadelphia, where, for several years, she resided as a leading actress. After a long absence from New York, she re-appeared at Laura Keene's theatre, in May, 1858, and in 1866, played a brilliant engagement at the Winter Garden."[7]

[7]Ireland, *op. cit,* II, 448-49.

For The United States Gazette[1]

Prologue

By David Paul Brown, Esq.
Spoken by W. Archer

To Mr. Smith's New Tragedy of Caius Marius

Imperious custom in her sovereign sway,
Enjoins a Prologue—or forbids the play.
Here, in her temple, who shall dare withstand
The awful thunders of her dread command;
Who scorn her fiat—who despise her pow'r,
He wakes the sleeping lion—to devour!
Submission only can success ensure,
And he thrives best that can the most endure.
Unmurmuringly, before her shrine I bend
To weave the votive chaplet for a friend,
To lead retiring genius into view,
Then leave its nurture and support to you;
To you the Poet—and his play submit,
You are his fates—Box, Gallery and Pit.

But give me leave—I have a word to say
Before we usher in the author's play;
Not to unfold his plot—and thus forestall
The joys of many, and the hopes of all;
Not to adorn the author—he, 'tis known,
Shines not in borrowed lustre—but his own;
But barely to premise, that should my muse,
The genial influence of her smile refuse,
The froward vixen in her wayward spleen,

[1]A printed clipping pasted in the ms. David Paul Brown, a friend of Smith and a fellow lawyer, was author of the play *Sertorius,* based on a theme closely related to that of *Caius Marius. Cf.* Introduction, p. 11. "Spoken by W. Archer" is interpolated in Smith's hand on the clipping. Arthur played Metellus in the production.

May fail to *mend*—but should not *mar* this scene,
Where native worth to native worth appeals,
And heart to heart, its sympathy reveals.
Enough of this—should we extend the lay,
The Prologue might be longer than the Play.

Marius again!—two thousand years have fled
Since Marius slumbered with the countless dead.
Now hoary time, his iron sceptre waves
O'er Rome—and Romans, one sad mass of graves;
Parent, and sons, all undistinguished lie,
Those whose ambition scaled the vaulted sky,
And fill'd the world with fame—now all repose
On classic earth—their virtues and their woes!
The eternal city! arrogant and vain,
Wrapt in oblivion's veil, shall ne'er again
Look from her seven-fold hills—and thence decree
Freedom to Slaves—and chains to Liberty!
Of Altars, Temples, Cenotaphs and Fanes,
Trophies and triumphs—what, alas, remains?
One common death surrounds great Caesar's tomb,
And Gods, and Heroes swell the gen'ral doom.

A Sepulchre is all that's left of Rome!
Who shall the great departed, dare recall,
Again to flourish, and again to fall?
What magic wand to hearts decay'd shall give
Warmth, impulse, action, till again they *live*—
Tear from its cerements, the dull prey of death,
And stimulate the breathless with a breath;
With plastic hand restore the mouldering flame,
To *form* and *feature,* and the soul reclaim;
Inspire new thoughts—fresh energies impart,
And stamp *old* Marius on *young* Forrest's heart.
Bid mighty Rome again, supreme; to rise,
To subjugate the world, and tempt the skies;
Revive her Senate with Promothean [*sic*] fire,
And Tully's hallowed lips again inspire;
Again attune Immortal Maro's lyre;
Who shall do this? This genius dares to do,

And all creation, and all *time* renew;
Exhaust the past—the future scene explore,
Till nature dies, and *genius is no more.*

[Ushers March]
Characters[1]

Caius Marius
Granius, his son
Metellus
Sulpitius
Sylla
Cinna
Antonius
A Cimbrian
Jugurtha, a mute
Martha, the sybil
Metella, daughter of Metellus
Servia

[1]On verso, facing the manuscript page of Act I, Scene 1, of the manuscript, the actors' parts are in the hand of Richard Penn Smith, their names in various hands in ink and pencil: Forrest, *Marius,* Smith, *Granius;* Archer, *Metellus;* Rowbotham, *Sulpitius;* Maywood, *Sylla;* Walton, *Cinna;* Porter, *Antonius;* Jones, A Cimbrian; at Albany, Bignaley to take the part; *Jugurtha, a mute* (no assignment); Mrs. Rowbotham, *Metella;* Martha, (unassigned); Miss Coleman, *Servia. Cf.* pp. 30-32 for the full cast.

Drum & Trumpet

Act 1.   Triumphal Arch

Scene 1.   A street in Rome. ✗✗ Shouts without. R.H.

Enter Sylla and Antonius meeting L.H.

Cinna and Metellus. R.H.

Metellus.	Sylla well met.
Sylla.	Metellus hail all hail t thee Metellus.
	The many headed monster has run mad.
	Hark to his brazen throat! Ay, there's a shout ✗✗ [Shouts loud
	To make Jove look and wonder at this pother.
Metellus.	The pride of Rome has fallen! Gods must it be
	A thing of yesterday, of little worth
	As the poor reptile in the compost bred,
	Should quicken thus and lord it o'er creation.
Sylla.	When the swoln Tiber foaming rages on
	The scum will evermore be on the surface.
Metellus.	Patricians' necks are footstools to his pride
	And must bend low to forward his ambition.

ACT I

SCENE 1

A street in Rome.[1] *Triumphal Arch. Shouts without. Enter Sylla and Antonius meeting Cinna and Metellus.*[2]

METELLUS Sylla, well met.

SYLLA   All hail to thee, Metellus.[3]
The many-headed monster has run mad.
Hark to his brazen[4] throat! Aye, there's a shout
 [Shouts, loud][5]
To make Jove look and wonder at this pother.

METELLUS[6] The pride of Rome has fallen! Gods, must it be *5*
A thing of yesterday, of little worth
As the poor reptile in the compost bred,
Should quicken thus and lord it o'er creation.

SYLLA When the swoln Tiber foaming rages on
The scum will evermore be on the surface. *10*

METELLUS Patrician necks are footstools to his pride
And must bend low to forward his ambition.

ANTONIUS Thy words are true as oracles, Metellus.
'Tis for thy conquests he obtains a triumph.
The glorious trophies by thy valor won; *15*
The royal captive of brave Sylla's hand,

---

[1]*Drum and Trumpet.*
[2][Sylla and Antonius enter from left, Cinna and Metellus from right.]
[3]L.1, canceled reading: "Metellus hail! All hail!"
[4]Canceled reading: "valorous"
[5][shouts from right]
[6][Metellus right center, Sylla left center]

	Compose the pageant that bloats up his fame	
	Almost to bursting.[7]	
SYLLA	His plumes are borrow'd, but the pompous daw	
	Shall yet be stripp'd of all his gaudy feathers.[8]	20
METELLUS	Sure Rome is drunk and frantic with her joy.	
	She sends forth numbers like a rolling deluge	
	To greet this would-be hero. All the ways,	
	Far as the eye can reach, on either side	
	Are lined with gaping crowds. On houses tops	25
	They cling like clustering bees; and ev'ry wretch	
	Who for offences long has been denied	
	The common benefits of sun and air,	
	Now leaves his hiding place and struts like a man.	
ANTONIUS	O! for the golden days when Scipio ruled	30
	The destinies of Rome. The people then	
	Enjoy'd their full extent of liberty.[9]	
	Nor had the nobles reason to complain,	
	For he himself was one.[10]	
METELLUS	But voices now are sold like merchandise.[11]	35
	And yet we boast of liberty. Just Gods!	
	That rulers of an empire should be chosen	
	By the wild clamour of a rabble rout	
	Where he who talks the loudest, and will drink,	

[7]Metellus as consul and then proconsul had repeatedly defeated Jugurtha, the leader of the Numidian forces in Africa, but had not been able to capture him or put his forces to final rout. In 107 B.C., Marius became consul and took over command from Metellus, his preceptor. Sylla, quaestor and later legate of Marius, had brought about the betrayal of Jugurtha by his father-in-law, but the fugitive was turned over to Marius who received the credit for the entire enterprise. The war ended with Marius' return to Rome with his prized captive, and the celebration of his triumph on January 1, 104 B. C.

[8]On facing page, *Shouts and Drum*

[9]Ll.31,32, canceled reading: " . . . The people's rights/ Were then within due bounds preserv'd, yet they"

[10]Antonius, a noble, recalled the patrician rule of Scipio Africanus Minor (185–129 B.C.), conqueror of Carthage.

[11]On the facing page, cue to Marius "MB for Triumphal Arch"

	From the same cup with foul-breath'd artizans[12] *40*
	Is hail'd a statesman fit to guide the world.

SYLLA

And this we owe to Marius; whose pride
Urged him to bribe the people for their votes
For consul in the war against Jugurtha.
And we all know, by what disgraceful arts   *45*
He robb'd you, brave Metellus, of your office
While your lieutenant, late in Africa.[13]

METELLUS

Gods! that a weed, sprung from a sterile soil,
Uncultur'd and neglected in the shade,[14]
Should proudly tower its head; defy the storm   *50*
And cast a shadow o'er the fate of Rome.

SYLLA

There's nought can curb the rage of his ambition,
But, like th' insatiate sea, the more 'tis fed[15]
By tributary streams, the wilder grows,
'Till having swallow'd all that earth can yield   *55*
It heaves with pride, and battles with the
    Gods.[16]

CINNA

Again he courts the people to be made
The leader of the forces raised to march
Against the King of Pontus.[17]

[12] Canceled reading: "citizens"; another hand in pencil: [foul-] "mouth'd demagogues"

[13] Marius had gone to Africa as the lieutenant of Metellus and there had won the admiration of the common soldiers. He aspired to the consulship, a heady ambition for a man of plebeian birth. After an open break with his commander over the fate of a family friend of Metellus, he repeatedly asked for leave to return to Italy to seek the consulship. Reluctantly, Metellus gave permission only ten days before the election. Marius crossed the sea in four days and easily won the election by promising to subdue Jugurtha.

[14] A reference to Marius' humble birth at Arpinum, about sixty miles southeast of Rome.

[15] Ll. 52-54, canceled reading: "The state already groans beneath the weight/ Of his ambition. Nought can curb its rage/ Which like the boundless sea" . . . /

[16] On facing page, *ready Wind Instruments*

[17] Mithridates IV had conquered the north coast of the Black Sea and in 88 B.C. declared war on Rome. At this time he had

ANTONIUS   Shall he triumph,[18]   60
While Sylla more deserving of the trust
Stands by neglected?[19]

METELLUS   By the Gods he shall not.
Rome now has staked her freedom on the die,
And we must play a desperate game to win it.
For should the chance be ours, he hides his head
And sinks forgotten e'en by those who raised
    him.   65
Flourish without.[20]

SYLLA   The roaring tide of cringing slaves moves on;
The air-blown bubble floats upon the surface
And apes the demi-god.[21]

METELLUS   Crack your swoln cheeks, ye sycophants and
    panders;
Rend the blue arch above with sounds
    discordant,   70
Until the merry gods send back the echo
With bursts of laughter at this mock parade.

SYLLA   Martha the sybil is with him.

METELLUS   As it should be
For in her wild predictions doth consist
His all of greatness.[22]   75

[Wind Instruments] The triumph enters.[23] *Captives, military and citizens. Marius drawn in his*

invaded Greece and Macedonia. The playwright has compressed
the time for dramatic effect; Marius' victorius return with Jugurtha was in 105 B.C.

[18] L.59, canceled reading: "Shall he have it,"

[19] Sylla, consul in 88 B.C. and aristocratic leader of the
senate, had been appointed commander against Mithridates, but
the populares, or democratic party, resisted and compelled the
senate to give the command to Marius.

[20] On facing page, *Shouts and Drum*

[21] *Shouts*

[22] *March Wind Instruments*

[23] ["R H U E (right hand upper entrance) through Arch"]

triumphal car; Jugurtha chained to the wheel.
Martha, dressed in a purple robe, with a spear[24]
in her hand, adorned with garlands, is carried on
a litter.

MARIUS Ye men of Rome and friends of Marius,
I am among ye once again, and I
Rejoice that I return not as I left ye.
If I was worthy of your favor, then,[25]
I trust I've proved myself still more deserving. *80*
Honors you heap'd upon me, more 'twas said,
Than my weak shoulders could support, but lo!
I have return'd, my back unbroken still;
And in your boundless prodigality[26]
Ye add unto the burden—Still I bend not, *85*
Though some did hope it might be otherwise
And brought their idle scorn to weigh me down;
But such must learn that Marius ne'er was born
To bend beneath their malice or[27] their blows;
And while devoted to the people's cause, *90*
A cause in which Feritrian[28] Jove takes part,
He will bear up though mountains fall to crush
 him.
They cannot crush if human rights sustain him.
Move on to the capitol.

 Shouts. Scene closes.[29]

[24]Canceled. In another hand in ink: "With a spear adorned
with garlands, in her hands." In pencil: "The spear adorned with
ribbons and Garlands." At the close of the directions, in Forrest's hand: *Flourish*

[25]Ll.79 through 82 bracketed in pencil but not canceled.

[26]On facing page, [Martha, center rear; Marius, mid-center;
Cinna, right front; Metellus, middle right; Sylla, middle left and
Antonius, left front]

[27]In another hand: [even] "less,"

[28]Wild, savage.

[29]On facing page, *Wind instruments;* on text page in another
hand: "March up through Arch and off"

SCENE 2

*An apartment in Metellus' house. Enter Metella
and Servia.*[1]

METELLA   Good Servia, is the triumph over yet?[2]

SERVIA   It is. I gazed until they reached the capitol.
                 When Marius descended form his car and entered.[3]

METELLA *(aside)*   Yet he comes not!

SERVIA   Did you speak?

METELLA   It was a brilliant sight, my Servia,
                                            Was it not?   *5*

SERVIA   It was, the like we ne'er may see again.[4]

METELLA   And yet it made me sorrowful, to see
                 A subjugated monarch thus exposed,
                 E'en as a common slave, to th' public gaze
                 Of those his valor once had fill'd with dread.   *10*
                 War is a frightful trade!

SERVIA   I've heard as much, and I have also heard
                 That woman's heart, as timid as it seems,
                 Is seldom frighten'd much by those who follow
                 it.

METELLA   Where can he linger! O, my Granius   *15*
                 Has absence then obliterated quite
                 Metella's fondness from thy memory!   *(Aside)*

SERVIA   How striking was the form of Marius!

[1]Interpolated, [Metella enters from right and Servia from left]

[2]L.1, canceled reading: "Is the triumph over, Servia, yet?"

[3]Ll.2,3, canceled reading: "It is, lady. I gazed after it until they reached the capitol. When Marius descended from his/ car. And entered, *(Shouts)* Heard you not the shout?"

[4]L.6, canceled reading: " 'Twas indeed, and such as we/ May never live to see again."

METELLA	All eyes were fixed upon him; and he look'd
	Like the huge statue of the God of War *20*
	That stands in the Campus Martius[5] —did he not?

SERVIA	Yet there was one whose manly bearing seem'd
	To please your eye far more.

METELLA	And who was that?

SERVIA	His son.

METELLA	Fie, fie! You exercise a woman's privilege
	And give more words than reason to your
	speech.[6] *25*

SERVIA	Perhaps I do, but *see,* your hero comes;
	Deny it to his face and I have done.

Enter Granius[7]

GRANIUS	Joy of my life, and summit of my hopes,
	With all the speed of anxious love I've flown,
	To hear those rosy lips again pronounce, *30*
	Metella still the same as when we parted.

SERVIA	She's still the same, yet if I judge aright
	Those blushes and that downcast look forbid
	The frank avowal.

METELLA	Why Servia!

SERVIA	Nay stand not thus; you surely do not see
	His arms extended ready to receive you. *35*

GRANIUS	Forgive me, blushing beauty, if my love
	O'erstep the bounds of prudence, and I dare
	With throbbing heart, thus seize the richest prize
	This world e'er proffer'd man.

METELLA	O! Granius!
	Joy at thy safe return makes me forget, *40*

[5]In northwestern Rome, an open area dedicated to Mars where armies trained and elections and other public functions were held.

[6][Metella crosses to the left.]

[7][Granius to enter from the left.]

The modesty that's due unto my sex,
While thus I welcome thee. *Embraces him*

SERVIA   And think you still
My speech had more of words than reason in
    it?[8]
I was once young myself; but time has blurred
    the record.

METELLA   I must confess you did not talk as idly   *45*
As I supposed.

SERVIA   Remember I was once
Of thy own age, and years you know bring
    wisdom.[9]

METELLA   How well he looks, good Servia! See that cheek
That once was rosy as an infant's palm
And quite as delicate, is now swath'd o'er   *50*
With a good manly colour; and these locks[10]
Are a shade darker, too. Now by my life
If I supposed the wars would thus improve
My beauty, I should be inclined to arm,
And serve a campaign or two abroad myself.[11]   *55*

GRANIUS   O! thou canst conquer more, e'en as thou art
Than arm'd with sword and buckler.

METELLA   Ha! turn'd courtier!
But tell me Granius all thy strange adventures;
How many thou hast slain in single fight;
How many captives made—and tell me true—   *60*
Both in the camp and court, for I would learn
If that same tender heart of thine has 'scap'd
Captivity, and now returns to me
Without a wound received from foreign eyes.

[8]L.43, canceled reading: "There were more words than reason
in my speech!"

[9]Ll.46,47, alternate reading on facing page: "I was of your
age once and years bring wisdom."

[10]Ll.50,51, canceled reading: "Is bronz'd with a manly
colour"

[11]In another hand, an alternative reading for "serve":
"follow"; "or two" canceled.

GRANIUS   O! I have much to ask and much to tell;   *65*
But with two female tongues employ'd against
   me,
I scarce can force a single word in edgewise.[12]

SERVIA   If you have much to say, begin not here;
Let us retire:—Her father might return
And interrupt us in the very pith   *70*
Of the story, and much I fear I'd die
                         Of curiosity.

METELLA   Let us retire then, for I would not be
An accessory to the death of this
Good creature. Come Granius come.

SERVIA   Here's a change!
"War is a frightful trade."—those were your
   words,   *75*
And yet you dread not to encounter one
Flush'd from the field of battle. How is this?

METELLA   It is the privilege of youth, you know,
To scorn all danger—Age, you say, brings
   wisdom.
Should I but live to be as old as thou   *80*
I'll be as wise and prudent, every whit.

SERVIA   Go in, thou arch one, in.

GRANIUS   How your tongues run.[13]   *(Exeunt)*

---

[12] Canceled in another hand: "to hearing" instead of "in edgewise."

[13] L.82, last sentence canceled; in pencil in another hand: "Come come Mettella [*sic*]"

SCENE 3

*A street in Rome before the Capitol. Enter Sylla
and Cinna, meeting.*[1]

SYLLA   The senate holds together long today.
The task is not easy, it would seem,
To check the pride of Marius.—What news!

CINNA   He will not yield a single point, resolv'd
To keep his ground or fall.

SYLLA   Then let him fall.   5

CINNA   Behold they come.[2]

Senators pass over the stage.[3]
Enter Metellus.

SYLLA   Your session has been long.

METELLUS   Far better that the senate ne'er should meet
Than patiently endure the insults of
The lowest born among us.

SYLLA   What has happen'd?

METELLUS   This newborn hero had conven'd the senate,   10
But too elated with the part he play'd
In the fantastic farce that shamed all Rome,
He entered, dress'd in his triumphal robes,
And took his seat among us.[4]

SYLLA   Bold as Mars.

---

[1] [Sylla to enter from the right and Cinna from the left.] On
facing page: "No more music"

[2] L.6, canceled; in another hand: "Metellus comes."

[3] Stage directions changed in another hand: "Enter Metellus
from the capitol."

[4] *Plutarch's Lives*, II, 251: "After the solemnity was over,
Marius assembled the senate in the capitol, where, either through
inadvertency, or gross insolence, he entered in his triumphal
robe, but soon perceiving that the senate was offended, he went
and put on his ordinary habit, and then returned to his place."

METELLUS   I raised my voice against the barefaced insult;   *15*
       Others soon follow'd, to compel the knave,
       To pay all due respect unto the senate.

CINNA   And what said he?

METELLUS   He made us no reply
       But smiled in scorn and sat immovable.

SYLLA   'Twas bold in you, for know you not, Metellus,[5] *20*
       His Syrian Sybil has long prophesied
       That he shall reign in Rome?

METELLUS   Not quite so bad!
       Seven times consul, nothing greater yet.[6]

CINNA   'Tis passing strange
       That one so young and gentle should devote *25*
       Her life to such a being. As well might[7]
       The dove become enamour'd of the tiger.

SYLLA   He saved her at the sacking of some town
       In Africa, and for that service, she
       Seems bound to him by more than mortal[8] ties. *30*

METELLUS   'Tis said he loves the girl!

SYLLA   And so he does;
       As much as such a man can love ought earthly.
       It is a passion that belongs alone
       To his peculiar nature.

---

[5] L.20, alternative reading in another hand: " . . . bold in him, ɔut know you not . . . . "

[6] A satiric reference to the prophecy which Marius often repeated, that when he "was very young, and lived in the country, an eagle's nest fell into his lap, with seven young ones in it. His parents . . . applied to the diviners, who answered, that their son . . . would seven times attain the highest office. . . ." *Cf. Plutarch's Lives,* II,271.

[7] Ll.26,27, alternative reading in another hand: "Her life to such a man. The dove as well might/ become enamour'd of the vulture."

[8] Canceled; in another hand: "human"

CINNA   See he comes.

Enter Marius from the capitol.

METELLUS Hail, to the conqueror of Jugurtha,[9] hail!   35
To the third founder of immortal Rome.[10]

SYLLA We greet your valor for the brilliant close
Put to the war in Afric.

MARIUS Thanks for your greeting if it merit thanks.

METELLUS How swift the restless wheel of Fortune turns!   40
I cannot but admire that thou'rt the same,
Who lately served in Afric, my lieutenant.

MARIUS Why pause you there.—Shall I proclaim the
rest?—
Then was elected consul o'er thy head,
And closed the war thy feebleness began.   45

METELLUS Thy memory is retentive, but I fear
A change of fortune may decrease its power.
Do not forget, while filled with mighty dreams,
That thy ambition which the world confines,
Once knew no world beyond a cottage wall.   50

MARIUS The greater praise is mine, who from the earth,
Unfoster'd, unprotected, like the oak,
Have tower'd towards the heavens, and gain'd
such strength.
The mighty in their places—the hot house plants,
Rear'd with such care, the fresh breeze pierces
them—   55
Look up with envy, while their sickly heads
Droop 'neath my shade. No genial ray can reach
them;[11]

[9] Alternative reading in another hand, for this phrase:
"Jugurtha's victor"

[10] A derogatory reference to the populace who, after Marius'
defeat of the Cimbri in 101 B.C., had hailed him the third founder of Rome. *Cf. Plutarch's Lives*, II, 263. The author is again
taking poetic license with the time sequence.

[11] L.57, last clause canceled, perhaps by the author.

They blossom'd for a day, 'tis time to wither.—
Hadst thou been born within a cottage—

METELLUS   Well!—

MARIUS   Within a cottage thou hadst surely died!—   *60*
Scoff at my birth!—I stand the work of Jove—
Thou scoff'st at him, not me. Proud man, scoff
        on;
I heed thee, as old Caucasus[12] would heed,
The melting influence of a summer breeze;
And thank the Gods e'en while thou scoff'st
        at me.   *65*

METELLUS   For what?

MARIUS   That I, sir, was not born to blush
For the dark deeds of my progenitors.
That I have no diseas'd and feeble mind
To prove that I am *honorably* descended.
May thy[13] posterity proclaim as much   *70*
With the same truth that I do.

SYLLA   He has great cause, indeed, to thank the Gods!

MARIUS   I cry you mercy. What says my lieutenant?

SYLLA   Thou hast more cause to thank the Gods,
              methinks
For having snatch'd thee from thy father's
              calling,[14]   *75*
Whose whole ambition was to rear a leek[15]
Or cultivate an herb.

MARIUS   You wrong his mem'ry much, he did far more;
He rear'd a son to do his country service,

---

[12]A personification referring to the lofty Caucasian Mountains.

[13]Canceled reading: "Your"

[14]*Plutarch's Lives,* II, 242: "His parents were obscure and indigent people, who supported themselves by labour. . . ."

[15]Canceled; in another hand: "flower"

| | And one who brooks no insult to his ashes.— | *80* |

And one who brooks no insult to his ashes.— *80*
Would thine had done the same.[16]

METELLUS
The hero is becoming splenetic;
Let us begone ere he grows scurrilous
And shows the rudeness of his origin.

MARIUS
The hint's well timed; the sinews of my sire[17] *85*
Were as unbending as this trusty blade;
Perhaps you may not feel dispos'd to test
The legitimacy of his son.[18]

SYLLA
We have not time to listen to your spleen.

Exeunt Met., Syl., and Cin., laughing[19]

MARIUS
The cur that shows his teeth will seldom bite. *90*
I know you all, and well I know if curses
Stuck to the back, ere this I had been blister'd.
I also know, if your most earnest prayers
Had weight above, ere this I'd been removed,
That ye might rule with iron heart and hand, *95*
And mount your thrones upon the neck of man.
But neither prayers nor curses shall avail!
I'll thwart your purpose yet.

Enter Sulpitius and guards.[20]

SULPITIUS
Halt, ye unruly rascals, halt, I say!
And tho' ye are unwilling to acknowledge *100*
Law in all Rome, I'd have ye quickly learn
My word's the law and there is no appeal.
So halt, I say.—How now, your temper's stirr'd.

MARIUS
Straws, straws, too fragile to inflict a wound
May goad to madness when th' incision's made. *105*

---

[16]On facing page, in another hand in pencil: *Ready Shout R & E*

[17][Marius to cross right.]

[18][Marius to cross left.]

[19][right hand exit.]

[20]*Shouts;* [In another hand, right entrance; centurions to enter with guards.]

SULPITIUS	I guess the cause, for even now I met,
	Livid faced Sylla, and his friend Metellus,
	In close discourse, and as they quickly pass'd
	Your name was mention'd, but a single glance
	At me and mine, who regulate the law, *· 110*
	By the strong rule of nature, was sufficient.—
	They hurried on without saluting us.

MARIUS	The world, Sulpitius, is quite large enough
	For honest men, but cannot hold us three.—
	We jostle as we pass. *115*

SULPITIUS	Then do as I do; no one jostles me.
	My body guard; my anti-senate here,[21]
	Composed of as choice spirits as e'er drain'd
	A flask, and when the wine was out drew swords,
	And fell to work upon each other's throats, *120*
	By way of pastime; these brave hearts I say
	Keep the way clear, and no one jostles me,
	Their tribune, consul, nay supreme dictator.

MARIUS	Your lawless ways give much offence in Rome.[22]

SULPITIUS	Marry to whom?

MARIUS	The nobles; the patricians. *125*

SULPITIUS	I do not question it. Two of a trade
	Will seldom praise each other, and 'tis said
	My lawless ways do not diverge so widely
	From the right path, but that they sometimes run
	Foul of the ways of our grave senators. *130*
	Am I to blame in this? You'll say I am;

---

[21] *Cf. Plutarch's Lives,* II, 269: "The commonwealth had been sickly for some time, and now her disorder came to a crisis. Marius had found a fit instrument for her ruin in the audacity of Sulpitius . . . he got six hundred men of the equestrian order about him as his guard, whom he called his *Anti-senate.*" The tribune Sulpitius proposed the law transferring the command against Mithridates from Sylla to Marius.

[22] Ll.124 through 137 cut in pencil.

But till my taste is chang'd and I prefer
Crawling in dust upon my hands and knees
To walking forth erect, like him who gave
The spirit that impels to venturous deeds,   *135*
I shall not change my ways altho' they prove
Offensive to the laws and the law makers.

MARIUS   My brave old soldier!

SULPITIUS   Follow my advice.
This Sylla and Metellus cross your path
At ev'ry turn; their engines are at work   *140*
To cause your downfall. Their first step will be
Sylla's election o'er your head to serve
Against the King of Pontus; and the next
Your death or exile.[23]

MARIUS   I care not for life;
'Tis but a tenure for my country's good   *145*
Which when recall'd, I'll freely render up
And shall not shrink when my account's
    examined.

SULPITIUS   I do not question it, but for my part
I'm in no haste to settle that account;
Nor would it be, sir, for the good of Rome   *150*
That you should render back your stewardship
At such a time as this. Look to the stake
We have upon the die.

MARIUS   Do not suppose
My eye has ever yet lost sight of it.
'Tis the divinity that I adore—   *155*
The bright-eyed goddess, Liberty—whose smiles
Like the red fire of Jove direct me through
This fierce and murky storm; nor will[24] I rest
Until I've burst the sacriligeous bonds

[23] Sulpitius is predicting the later effort on the part of Marius
to wrest control of the Mithridatic campaign from Sylla, whose
successful attack against the forces of Marius compelled the old
general to flee Italy and take refuge in Africa.
[24] Canceled; in another hand: "will"

That bind her agile limbs, and they are free,   *160*
As when she first came down to bless mankind.

SULPITIUS   All eyes are on you, and the people hope
To see their ancient rights again restored.

MARIUS   The people are the fountain of all power[25]
Which springing from that source, direct, is pure,   *165*
But when cut off—the stream confin'd within
A narrow channel it becomes corrupt—
A wild destructive torrent that o'erwhelms
Whate'er oppose its fury. Yes, my friend,
The people's rights must be restor'd to them[26]   *170*
But no mild measures can effect that end.

SULPITIUS   I will again propose th' agrarian law,[27]
All cry aloud for it.

MARIUS   But with such feeble tongues
The infant Liberty sleeps undisturb'd.
If one had but the manhood to stand forth   *175*
And vindicate his nature, tyranny
Would tremble in her seat, and e'en[28] our lords
Who as they pass the streets in full flown pride,
Disdain the honest artisans they meet
As the base earth they tread on—Even they   *180*
Would feel their inborn littleness, and shrink
Beneath the frown of those they rule with
     scourges.—
All, say you, cry aloud? go on, go on.

SULPITIUS   I will again propose the agrarian law,
And call upon the senate to come forth,   *185*
And swear, in full assembly, to confirm
Whate'er the people shall decree, as law.[29]

[25] Ll.164 through 169 cut in ink.
[26] L.170, "must" cancelled; in another hand, "shall"; "to them" canceled.
[27] Ll.172 through 183 cut in pencil, l.183 in ink.
[28] Canceled; in another hand: "even"
[29] Saturninus, a tribune before Sulpitius, had proposed this law which called for grants of land to non-Roman Italians who

MARIUS   Gall to the palate, gall, by Hercules![30]
Bend your unwilling necks, ye proud patricians,
And learn that in the midst of all your pomp,   *190*
And vain display of ill-got, misus'd wealth
Man still is man and nought can change his
     nature.

SULPITIUS   Metellus ne'er will bend his neck to this.

MARIUS   Then his stiff neck must break beneath the
     weight.
Haste, haste, Sulpitius, ere the matter cool.   *195*
But look to the clause; let it with care be
     worded,
That subtle wits may not evade the meaning.
I'll to the senate and assist your purpose.
Look to the clause; write it in flame, Sulpitius.
Or with the deadly point of thy good sword,   *200*
That it may poison vile patrician throats
That utter it. Look to the clause, I say.

       exeunt
        End of Act I[31]

---

had fought with Marius, a law naturally opposed by the Roman
patrician party. The demand that the senate should swear to
confirm what the people would request was resisted by the
aristocratic senate. Marius, by seeming to agree with the senate
(*cf,* Act II, Scene 1), actually sided with the people, thus forcing
the senate to follow his vote. Metellus, however, refused and
accepted banishment to Rhodes (*cf. Plutarch's Lives,* II, 264-66)
and did not suffer the fate assigned to him in this play.

[30]Ll.188 through 198 cut in pencil.

[31][Marius exits left, Sulpitius, centurions and guards exit
right, and Marius changes dress.]

ACT II

SCENE 1

The Senate, Marius, Metellus, Antonius and Senators.

ANTONIUS   You've heard the law just read. What are your
        voices?
     Shall we consent?

METELLUS   No, conscript fathers, no—
     While I have sense of man's prerogative;
     Know what is due unto the senate's wisdom,
     I ne'er shall place a scourge in madmen's hands;   *5*
     Strip off the robe of proud authority,
     And swear the people's voice immaculate.
     Altho' th' infectious breath offends the Gods.
     Not while there's manhood in me.

MARIUS   Bravely spoken!

METELLUS   And who is he that thus would strip the senate?   *10*
     A man, who springing from the basest earth
     With heart surcharged with envy—deadly hate,
     Would pull down all above him to his grade;
     A man, whose object is to raise a storm,
     That he may guide the warring elements,   *15*
     And having nought to lose himself, may share
     The wreck of others fortunes.— Yes; a man—

MARIUS   Who dares maintain his rights before the world
     And will not calmly sleep beneath his wrongs.
     A man who feels that even[1] the abject slave,   *20*
     Whose limbs are crimson'd by the lash of power,
     Inherits as his birthright from great Jove,
     A spirit free—possessed of equal claims

---

[1] Canceled; in another hand: "even"

And those who strut in the Attalic[2] robes,
As if they found not in their haughty breasts,   *25*
One sense in common with the lowly thing,
Their tyranny has made.

ANTONIUS   Your tongue's too bold.

METELLUS   He would betray the senate to the people.

MARIUS   Rather protect the people from the senate,
And break the iron yoke that binds their necks.—   *30*
Nay, start not yet, for I've more wholesome truths
To make your seats less easy. All the earth,
Her kings and tetrarchs are our tributaries;
People and nations pay us hourly stipends;[3]
The riches of the world flow into Rome   *35*
And yet we find the public coffers drain'd.
The commonwealth has been a common drab;
Ye use her for the basest purposes
And riot in her shame.

METELLUS   Ha! whither would this tend?

MARIUS   It strikes my soul—   *40*
And who can 'scape the stroke[4] that hath a soul?—
To see you swell with treasures not your own,
And pour out in your idle luxuries
The revenue of kingdoms.—All this while
The people are kept trembling 'neath your rods   *45*
With scarce sufficient bread, or wherewithal
To give their naked bodies covering.—

[2] A slighting reference to the Romans who were proud of their long protectorate over the Attalid dynasty, powerful in northwest Asia Minor from 300 B.C., who provided the pretext for the intervention of Rome into Grecian life by means of the Macedonian wars. The Attalid dynasty ended in 133 B.C., and its possessions were bequeathed to Rome, thus bringing advantage to the already privileged classes.

[3] Ll.34 through 39 bracketed in pencil and in the margin in another hand: "Ben Jonson". The lines are almost verbatim from Jonson's *Catiline,* Act I, ll.349-53.

[4] Canceled: in another hand: "to blow"

You buy rare Attic statues, Tyrian hangings,[5]
Ephesian pictures and Corinthian plate;
The Phasis and the Lucrine Lake[6] are search'd   50
To please the palate dull with gluttony;
Your ancient habitations you neglect,
And set up new, then if the echo fail,
You choose another site and build again.
All frantic ways are used to waste Rome's wealth   55
While we are kept as if we were your slaves
With scarce a fire or e'en a Lar[7] to worship.
And why is this?—I put the question home,
And call the Gods to witness that the power
Is in our hands—Let not the truth alarm you—   60
Our limbs are able and our minds are strong.—
But with your noble order—Look and blush—
All things have sunk with luxury and years,
And ye are scarce the phantoms now of men.
Let but this glorious work be once begun—[8]   65
The issue's certain.

METELLUS   Treason to the senate.

MARIUS   Justice to the people!
I come not here to speak our grievances
In honied accents and with tongue of oil.
Too long our loud complaints have been
     unheard,   70
And we, in tones of thunder must proclaim
The people's voice is here omnipotent;
And as from them all power originates,
Into their hands all power must be return'd.

[5] Ll.48 through 64 bracketed and in the margin in another hand in pencil: "Ben Jonson". These lines, again, are almost direct quotations from Jonson's *Catiline*. Act I, Ll.384-396.

[6] The Phasis (now the Rion River), main stream of West Georgia in Russia, emptying into the Black Sea and carrying rich supplies of fish; Lake Lucrino, a coastal lake in Campania, noted for oysters.

[7] Lar, the spirit who had particular care of the household and was worshiped as a kind of familial deity.

[8] L.65, canceled reading: "There wants but only to begin the work."

The law to this effect you all have heard;   75
Your oaths are wanting to maintain the law.[9]
The people have assembled in the forum
Now to receive and register your oaths.
'Tis meet you there adjourn and render up
The trust you have so shamefully betray'd.   80

METELLUS   Who is here base enough to take the oath?

MARIUS   Who is here bold enough to hesitate!
Ye have gone on until ye've roused the lion,
Take warning at the thunder of his voice
Ere ye provoke him to employ his talons—   85
On to the forum!—on!—

        exeunt

SCENE 2

A street.   Enter Sulpitius followed by citizens.[1]

SULPITIUS   What do ye from the forum, citizens,
At such a time when Liberty's at work?
Ha! know ye not the senate have come forth
To tell ye what perhaps ye never knew;
They were not born with bucklers on their backs, 5
Pikes in their hands, and cuirass on[2] their breasts,
Sent ready arm'd, as by the grace of Jove
Into this world to ride your necks at pleasure.

1ST CITIZEN   A marvellous discovery my masters.

SULPITIUS   Well strange as it may seem, they did not find   10
It out till now. And it required some words

[9] A reference to the specific clause in the newly proposed agrarian law stipulating that the senate must swear to uphold whatever the populace voted. This was a democratic action contrary to the Roman custom but obviously favored by the common men.

[1] [Matrons are included in the scene and all enter from the right.]

[2] "Cuirass on" canceled; in another hand: "shields upon"

To prove the fact. Ha! neighbor, by this light
Thou hast a jolly face; a rosy face,
And now I look again, a comely face.

1ST CITIZEN 'Tis well enough, sir, for a botch—a cobbler. *15*

SULPITIUS A cobbler say you! You abuse your worth.
Throw down your lapstone,[3] and pray botch no
 more.
Thou art a lord; a nobleman! I' faith
The senate has proclaim'd thee such a man;
Quite equal to the proudest in all Rome— *20*
And who dare doubt the wisdom of the senate.

 Citizens laugh

1ST CITIZEN Our worthy tribune is a merry man.

SULPITIUS But that good face! It strikes me I have seen
That face before.

1ST CITIZEN As oft as there are stitches in your sandals; *25*
For my poor stall is at the foot of your worship's
 garden.

SULPITIUS I know you now. Go home and thank Jove that
I'm a bachelor; for were I a married man
Thou shouldst cobble no longer at the foot of
 my garden,[4]
I'll warrant you.—That face, that jolly face, *30*
Will be your ruin. *Citizens laugh.* Now hasten
 to the forum,
And as you walk along, cry out for Marius.[5]
 exeunt citizens.
The work goes bravely on. Here come a brace
Who have no appetite for what is doing.

 Enter Cinna and Sylla[6]

---

[3] A stone, held in the lap, on which cobblers beat leather.
[4] In the manuscript, Ll.26,27, and 28 ran on without regard
for metrical line and punctuation.
[5] *Shouting* [and initials to indicate right exit]
[6] [Cinna follows Sylla on stage from the left.]

SYLLA   Behold his satellite! We here may learn   *35*
               Who still are faithful to us.—Worthy tribune?—

SULPITIUS *(Aside)*   My merits are discover'd; in good time, too!
               I yesterday was called a cut-throat knave,
               But now their eyes are open'd and I prove
               A worthy tribune.—Well, my noble friends—   *40*
               For still I may presume to call you noble—
               A happy day to both and a right merry one.

CINNA   The same to you. Pray, come you from the
                    forum?

SULPITIUS   Straight.[7] When I say straight, I mean,
               Straight as a man can come whose shoulders bend *45*
               Beneath the weight of honour heap'd upon them
               By the just senate.

SYLLA   Have all ta'en the oath?

SULPITIUS   The sport is not quite over; if you haste
               You yet may see enough to make you merry.

SYLLA   Has old Ancharius[8] sworn?

SULPITIUS   I' faith, he has.[9] *50*
               The oath, I must confess, went nigh to choak
                    [*sic*] him.
               It stuck in his throat, crosswise, and would not
                    stir,
               When I in pity smote him on the back,
               And out it bolted.

CINNA   It was kindly done.

SULPITIUS   And yet he did not thank me.   *55*

SYLLA   Antonius—has Antonius ta'en the oath.

SULPITIUS   Yes; as a sick man takes a dose of physic.
               He made wry faces and then swallow'd it.—

[7] [Sulpitius to cross to center]
[8] A senator later slain by Marius. *Cf. Plutarch's Lives*, II, 277.
[9] On facing page: *Ready Shouts R & H*

'Twill do him good, and purge him of his pride.

SYLLA   Metellus has not sworn?

SULPITIUS   Thou 'rt right, he has not.   60
But I will swear that ere tomorrow morn
He will find out he had much better sworn
A deeper oath than was requir'd of him,
Than to have roused the new made lords of
     Rome.
But, friends, I fear I keep you from the sport.   65
Along with me and I will find ye places
Among the sweet-breath'd sweating artisans,
Who will not scorn ye tho' they're just ennobled
And rais'd above your heads. Along with me.

CINNA *(Aside)*   Sarcastic dog!

SULPITIUS   Why do you hesitate?   70
They'll treat you as their equal never fear;
Along[10] with me and I'll secure you places.
     (exit)[11]

SYLLA   Metellus is an honor to our order
And every noble should gird on his arms
To shield him from the fury of the mob.   75
Haste, Cinna, haste; call all our friends together
And bid them hold themselves in readiness
In this dark hour of peril.

CINNA   I'll about it. *exeunt*[12]

---

[10] [cross right]
[11] [right exit]
[12] [Cinna to exit left and Sylla right]

SCENE 3

An apartment in Marius' house. Enter Marius.[1]

MARIUS

The storm is fairly up, and I must bare
My bosom to its fury, like Jove's bird
And sail aloft nor[2] wink not tho' the fire
Of heaven flash across[3] my aching sight.
The storm is fairly up, and shall not cease   *5*
'Till Rome stands forth regenerate and free.
And when the mighty vision that my brain
Now teems with is fulfill'd—when I behold
Th' elastic spirit rise, conscious of worth;
Hear man assert before th' assembled world   *10*
That freedom is his birthright—then great Jove
Thy shaft may strike;—I ask no more.—Who's
   there.

Enter Martha

MARTHA

May I disturb your privacy?

MARIUS

                                   Come in.
My little[4] smiling prophetess, come in.
The music of thy voice may lull to sleep   *15*
The tempest of my mind.

MARTHA

                                You seem disturb'd.

MARIUS

We've[5] launch'd our barque upon a stormy sea.

MARTHA

Yet[6] sail together.

---

[1] [Marius enters from the left; shouts are heard from the right.]

[2] Canceled: "and"

[3] Canceled; in another hand: "to sear"

[4] Canceled; in another hand: "tender"

[5] L.19 canceled; in another hand: "We've our barque launch'd upon a stormy sea."

[6] Canceled; in another hand: "We"

MARIUS	Right my Syrian girl!
	Let the sun shine, or let the tempest rise,
	We sail together and there's much in that. 20

MARTHA   Much—*all* to me!

MARIUS   Thou gentle and devoted one,
            Thou hast the talisman to wake to life
            The fondest feelings of my earlier days,
            In all their freshness.—O, thou art to me
            As the last born is to the aged sire!   25
            The holy flame that thou hast kindled here
            Is pure as that the spotless vestal guards,
            Though slightly stain'd by dregs of earthly
                matter.

MARTHA   Would it were not thus stain'd! But evermore
            Man's passions will partake of this base world,   30
            And he whose deeds should emulate the Gods,
            Sinks far beneath his nature.

MARIUS   The Greek Gods mean you.
            Such as we read of in their poets' dreams.

MARTHA   Each nation pictures heaven to please itself,
            And hopes to find its own peculiar joys   35
            Reviv'd there in a never dying state.—
            Because in painting those Elysian scenes,
            Their poets could conceive no joys beyond
            Our earthly pleasures, and have cloth'd their
                gods
            With human passions—sensual appetites,   40
            It does not follow that their dreams are true.

MARIUS   It does not follow.[7]

MARTHA   But admit them true.
            Then should our deeds be in this nether world
            Such as we'd gladly have again revive.

MARIUS   Well, mine are such as I would have revive.   45

[7]On facing page: *Shouts ready, L.*

MARTHA	Far better make them such as ne'er can die.
MARIUS	Nay now you ask too much. Do not forget That e'en the pious Numa[8] was but man; He wooed the sylph Egeria in the grove, And the stern Brutus[9] has his sybil, too.

50

MARTHA	But I would have thee more, far more than either A Brutus or a Numa; and if there's ought Prophetic in my mind, thou'lt be remembered Among the benefactors of mankind.

MARIUS	Thus would I be remember'd; but I fear There's more of sylph than sybil in thee, girl. Thy prophecy will never be fulfill'd.

55

MARTHA	Sylph or sybil as I am I'm thine, Nor would I be ought else to make this world My own.

MARIUS	True, thou art mine, nor would I have Thee otherwise to make this world my own.

60

Enter Sylla in haste, his sword drawn.[10]

SYLLA	I fly but know not where. O! bloody fiends! I shall be butcher'd by the common herd And die a death that ill becomes a soldier.[11]

---

[8] According to legend, Numa was the benevolent successor to Romulus as king of Rome, aided by Egeria, goddess of fountains and childbirth, who gave the king counsel at night by her sacred spring from which the Vestals drew water.

[9] Lucius Junius Brutus, who ended the tyranny of the Tarquinian kings and became the first consul of the Roman Republic in the sixth century B.C., had consulted the oracle at Delphi who predicted his ultimate rise to power.

[10] [Sylla enters from left.]

[11] "One day, while the consuls were holding an assembly of the people, Sulpitius came upon them with his assassins. The consuls immediately fled, but he seized the son of one of them, and killed him on the spot. Sylla (the other consul) was pursued, but escaped into the house of Marius, which nobody thought of; and when the pursuers were gone by, it is said that Marius himself let him out at a back gate, from whence he got safe to the camp." *Plutarch's Lives*, II, 269.

MARIUS   Sylla beneath my roof!

SYLLA   O! cursed chance!
I've sought the lion's den[12] in hopes of safety.   *65*
I'm in the toils, but I will show him sport
Ere I am taken.

MARIUS *(to Martha)* You may retire. *exit Martha*
                        Sylla, put up your sword—
You cannot mean to play the ruffian here.

SYLLA   Nor to be tamely slaughter'd.

MARIUS   Ha! by whom?

SYLLA   Thee and thy myrmidons.

                            You surely rave!   *70*
Is there not more of soldier in thy spirit,
Than to suppose that Marius e'er could take
A coward's vantage of his rankest foe.

SYLLA   Then why was I so dastardly beset,
And must have shared[13] the fate of many
        friends,   *75*
Had I not fled?

MARIUS   Ha! when was this?

SYLLA   But now.

MARIUS   By whom?

SYLLA   Sulpitius and his lawless partisans,
Who evermore are wand'ring through the streets,
Creating brawls and shedding noble blood.

MARIUS   Put up your sword—nay; prythee put it up.   *80*

SYLLA   What warrant have I that my life is safe?

MARIUS   The roof thou art beneath.
Thou'st sought my fireside in extremity—

---

[12]Canceled; in another hand: "Lair"

[13]L.75 "must have shared" canceled; in another hand: "doom'd to share"

He who would wrong a hair upon thy head
Must lop these limbs off first.

SYLLA   Can this be Marius!

MARIUS   Why question it?

SYLLA   I am your foe, surrounded by your friends   85
And in your power.

MARIUS   Not here; not here.
In this brief space my rule is absolute;
Beyond that door our lordly tyrants stalk[14]
Who deal out laws to sap the springs of life,
And crush the energies of prostrate man.   90
I've studied hard to keep their cursed rule
From passing o'er that threshold; do not think,
That I would imitate the thing I hate,
And play the tyrant here. You are at home.

SYLLA   I sheathe my sword, and with it half my hate.   95

MARIUS   Would thou could'st sheath thy wild ambition,
      too.

SYLLA   It is a godlike principle that stamps[15]
The human mind and fairly tests its value.
No heart in Rome has listen'd to its voice
More eagerly than thine.

MARIUS   I am ambitious!   100
To see content dwell round the cheerful hearth
And know that nought dare enter to disturb
The calm repose of those who nestle there;
This the extent of my ambitious hopes;
The noblest flight ambition ever took.   105

      Noise without[16]

SYLLA   What noise is that?

[14] Ll.88 through 92 cut in pencil.
[15] On facing page, *Shouts ready L H*
[16] *Shouts*

MARIUS   The steps of your pursuers.
In that apartment you will find a cloak[17]
That may disguise your person. Hence—away.
Pursue your course through my extended garden,
And you may pass the city unobserv'd.   *110*
Away! no thanks, for they may cost your life.

 Exit Sylla. Enter Granius, Sulpitius and his
 party.[18] Soldiers.

MARIUS   How now; what means this riotous intrusion!
Does Bacchus and his drunken crew approach?
To keep their horrid Saturnalia here?[19]
Is this a place for your disgraceful orgies?   *115*
And you, my son; is this act worthy him
Who from a love of justice should maintain
The rights of his worst foes? I blush for ye—
Hence, from my sight, my swarth cheek burns
 with shame.

 Exeunt all but Sulpitius and Marius

You are too sanguinary. This bloody course   *120*
Will bring disgrace upon us, and arouse[20]
The fears of those we struggle to protect.
'Tis not the way t' achieve the end we aim at.

SULPITIUS   It is the way; the surest and the shortest.

MARIUS   No human laws can firmly be maintain'd   *125*
While those divine are madly trampled on.

SULPITIUS   I will not thwart you, but you may regret
This lenity to Sylla, who would have
Remember'd longer a thrust through the heart,
And been as grateful.

MARIUS   I have done my duty.   *130*

 [17]Variant reading: "robe"
 [18][Sylla to exit left, and the "party" is to be made up of
centurions and soldiers.]
 [19]L.114, canceled.
 [20]Canceled reading: "excite"

SULPITIUS   And so has he; in every street you'll find
              His friends in arms.

MARIUS   And where is old Metellus?

SULPITIUS   Just taken leave to vegetate abroad.
              The new made lords escorted him in hundreds
              To the Flaminian gate.[21]

MARIUS   True he was proud   *135*
              But Rome, I fear, has not his equal left!

SULPITIUS   The better her estate.
              There's nought to hinder your election now.
              So to the forum where the citizens
              Await, impatient to proclaim you consul.   *140*

MARIUS   I will but get my sword and then attend you.[22]

              exeunt[23]

MARIUS   I stand upon the narrow line which past
              Enrolls my name with those that ne'er can die
              But how succeeding ages may adjudge
              No mortal can unriddle—none control.   *145*
              Oh Fame at best thou'rt but a game of chance
              Our deeds unremembered and our motives lost,
              The hazards equal whether we receive
              The execrations, or the applause of men.[24]

---

[21]Leading to the Via Flaminia, the road built in 220 B.C., crossing the Apennines to Rimini.

[22][Sulpitius to exit left. Added note: "Soliloquy Marius" and "Marius changes dress"]

[23]The following soliloquy added at the request of Forrest, in whose hand it is transcribed. *Cf.* Introduction, pp. 21-22.

[24]*Exit R H*

ACT III

SCENE 1

A room in Marius' house. Enter Marius and Sulpitius.[1]

MARIUS 'Tis done, and I am consul once again,
But mother Rome still heaves convulsively
As though she had produced some monstrous birth,
And not a son to honor and sustain her.

SULPITIUS Her throes will soon subside; but should they last *5*
I recommend phlebotomy—there's nothing
Like it in cases such as this. Let blood;
I'll be her surgeon.

MARIUS   Practice first on me.

Enter Martha[2]

MARTHA I greet thee as the consul still.

MARIUS   I thank thee—
What ails thee, child? By the twin gods[3] I know not *10*
Whether you smile or weep.

MARTHA   Both smile and weep.
Yet my o'erflowing joy's unmix'd with grief.

SULPITIUS I am not given much to poetry,
Or I would say she does not look unlike
An opening flower sprinkled with morning dew. *15*

---

[1] [left entrance]

[2] [right entrance]

[3] Castor and Pollux, twin gods in the Greek pantheon, particularly favored by the Romans.

MARIUS   Few flowers, Sulpitius, few as fair as this
Spring in a soldier's pathway.

SULPITIUS   None in mine, thank Venus!

MARTHA   Thy simile is threadbare.

SULPITIUS   Somewhat worn
But none the worse for wear. 'Tis one of those
That will pass current with the tuneful tribe   20
While women weep, and flowers drink morning
    dew.
I heard it used but yesterday, and aptly.

MARTHA   Pray, by whom?

SULPITIUS   By Silius the poet[4] —he whose lines
Are stuck upon the statues in the streets,
For popular applause. In passing by   25
His door, I saw his Hecate[5] of a wife
In tears. I paused; the poet turn'd to me
And pointing at her, with unusual warmth
Pour'd forth the speech that I have just repeated.

MARTHA   So 'tis but second hand then after all;   30
And I may read it in the streets tomorrow.
But where's the point? You said 'twas aptly used.

SULPITIUS   O! I remember! 'Twas a painful point!
I since have learnt he beat her for th' occasion,
And that, he said, was writing after nature.   35

MARTHA   Forever cynical!

MARIUS   He's privileged.
What better could you look for in a bachelor
Of fifty-five?

---

[4]Tiberius Catius Asconius Silius Italicus (*ca.* A.D. 25-101), consul in the last year of Nero's reign, lived in retirement in his later years and wrote the epic, *Punica,* a narrative in seventeen books of the Second Punic War. The playwright has again ignored the time sequence, in having Sulpitius refer to a poet yet unborn at the time of the action of the play.

[5] A Greek goddess who became associated with ghosts, magic, and witchcraft.

MARTHA   Not much, I must confess.[6]
But I have heard that he was once sweet-
    temper'd—
What has sour'd him?

MARIUS   The story is soon told.   *40*
In our first service under Scipio
He took a fancy to a sutler's wife,
Which coming to her angry husband's ears
He drubb'd him soundly with a crabtree stick,
And ever since his temper has been sour'd.   *45*
The crab-tree bears a bitter fruit, you know?

MARTHA   Sulpitius best can answer thee, for that.
Ne'er rail at woman in my presence more.

SULPITIUS   'Tis but a soldier's story, and requires
The aid of time and distance to insure   *50*
Credence among the credulous. He jests.

MARIUS   Deny it not.

    Enter Granius[7]

GRANIUS   There's one in waiting, cloth'd in weeds of woe
Desires to be admitted to your presence.

MARIUS   Who is it boy?

GRANIUS   I've said 'tis one that's wretched—   *55*
Thy door was never closed upon affliction.

MARIUS   Go—show the mourner in.—

    Exit Granius and returns with Metella[8]

GRANIUS   She's here.

MARIUS   Was this well done!

SULPITIUS   The daughter of Metellus!

---

[6] Ll.38 thru 52 cut in pencil.
[7] [left entrance]
[8] [Metella to enter from the left]

METELLA *(kneels)* Lo! bending at thy feet, with stricken heart
Behold a suppliant child. I kneel to thee   *60*
And trust to Nature's all persuasive voice
To plead my cause.

MARIUS   Rise, rise, fair mourner.

METELLA   I may not till thy lips pronounce my doom;
For life and death are in thy accents now.
I plead for one who served his country well,   *65*
And yet that country cast him off—disowns:—
The voice of youth in trembling accents breathes,
To ask compassion for the frail and old.
A daughter pleads for mercy for her sire
And can that plea be ever[9] urged in vain.   *70*

SULPITIUS   He wavers, by the Gods! *Marius raises her.*

METELLA   I ask but this—
That the dim embers of a brilliant life,
Ere now a beacon for its country's good,[10]
May claim as its reward the simple right
Of mouldering into ashes, undisturb'd.   *75*

SULPITIUS   Remember Rome.

GRANIUS   Rome may be free
And have Metellus still within her walls.

SULPITIUS   You echo but the sorrows of his child.

GRANIUS   You knew his worth—few knew his worth so
well,
And oft thy tongue has spoken in his praise—   *80*

MARIUS   I may not hear you more—You strike my soul.[11]
But cannot enter here.—You may awake
In vivid colours all Rome owes to him;

[9] L.70 altered in another hand: "Can that appeal be ever . . . ."
[10] L.73, canceled reading: "Devoted wholly to its country's good"
[11] Ll.81 through 93 cut in pencil.

	But there's no Lethe[12] to make me forget	
	What I still owe to Rome.[13]	85

MARTHA Art thou not blest with me?

MARIUS   What folly now!
Thou silly thing, thou knowest well[14] I prize
  thee.

MARTHA Yet there is not that sacred tie between us
That nature planted in her gentle breast
And her poor father's.—Still the loss of thee   90
I never could survive. Then think of her.

MARIUS So often hast thou travell'd to my heart
Each avenue is known to thee. No more.[15]

MARTHA He was your friend—when you required a
  friend—
I've heard you say so often.

MARIUS   So he was—   95
By all the gods he was:—but that is past.

MARTHA *He* now requires a friend!

SULPITIUS   And so does Rome.

MARIUS Ye torture me!

MARTHA   The brightest attribute of power
Is mercy. He who rules and bars his heart
Against its holy dictates,[16] turns awry   100
An ever-flowing fountain of delight,
And imitates the fiends, before he's cross'd
The Stygian lake.[17] But he who listens to
Its gentle tones, but imitates the gods;

[12] A river in Hades where those about to be reincarnated drank to insure forgetfulness of a previous existence.

[13] On facing page, *Drums and Trumpet*

[14] Canceled reading: "how"

[15] Canceled reading: "Be still"

[16] Canceled reading: "accents"

[17] Referring to the River Styx in the underworld over which souls of the dead were ferried by Charon.

	Dispensing good—where'er he chance to move	*105*
	He calls forth blessings from his fellow man	
	And feels himself the favorite of Jove.[18]	
SULPITIUS	Let mercy then be shown to Rome at large	
	And not confine it to a single man.	
METELLA	That dreadful voice! It freezes all my blood!	*110*
	If thou wert on the scaffold, and the axe	
	Ready suspended o'er thy head, and thou	
	Didst see a friendly hand stretch'd forth to save;	
	Wouldst thou not deem it was a savage act,	
	In him who thrust th' imploring hand aside,	*115*
	And coldly bade the uplifted weapon fall?	
SULPITIUS	Not if the word came from the lips of Justice.	
METELLA	There is no hope as long as he is nigh!	
MARIUS	I must begone, ere I betray my cause. *going*[19]	
METELLA	Ah! stir not yet, until thy word is given.—	*120*
	It is to save a father's life I strive.—	
MARIUS	And I to save my country.	
METELLA	Stir not yet.	
MARIUS	You plead in vain.	
	My heart weeps tears of blood for thee, poor child.[20]	
	And tho' one little word might heal thy woes,	*125*
	I may not utter it. All private griefs	
	Be merged in public good.	
METELLA	My father—save my father!	
MARIUS	The air grows wondrous close—I scarce can breathe.	
	I must go forth. Farewell poor innocent,	
	I pity thee, but dare not now relieve.[21]	*130*

[18] Canceled reading: "Heaven"
[19] [Marius to move right]
[20] Ll.124 through 127 cut in pencil.
[21] L.130, canceled reading: ". . . but I dare not relieve."

METELLA   Remember heartless man, the time may come
                 When you may plead for mercy too in vain.

                 Exeunt Marius and Sulpitius and scene closes[22]

                          S C E N E   2

                 A street.   Enter Marius and Sulpitius[1]

MARIUS   I breathe again; I breathe again! The air[2]
                 Plays far more freely here. I breathe again!
                 My heart is rugged, but I must confess
                 It ne'er beat freely mid a woman's sighs.

SULPITIUS   'Tis not the atmosphere for soldiers hearts.   *5*

MARIUS   My son and that fair mourner love, and[3] I
                 Deplore it, since their love must terminate
                 In bitterest woe.

SULPITIUS   Woe is the common destiny of love.

MARIUS   Has Sylla reached the army?

SULPITIUS   So I learn.   *10*

MARIUS   What answer bring the tribunes who were sent
                 Bearing my orders that he should deliver
                 The forces forthwith to them?

SULPITIUS   They are silent.
                 And ten to one will hold their peace forever.[4]

MARIUS   Have they turn'd traitors, too?

SULPITIUS   Not so, not so,   *15*
                 Their dumb and gaping wounds speak plainer far

_____

[22] [Right exit and Metella exits left.]
[1] [Right entrance]
[2] Ll.1 through 9 cut in pencil.
[3] "and" canceled; in another hand, the phrase to read: "much
do I"
[4] Ll.14 through 19 cut in pencil.

	Than living tongues could speak, that they were true.
MARIUS	Slain, mean you slain?[5]
SULPITIUS	Ay, hunted from the camp And stoned to death.[6]
MARIUS	Their blood shall be remember'd.

SULPITIUS The soldiers have espoused the cause of Sylla[7] 20
Unmindful that the laurels on their brows
Were planted by your hands.

MARIUS   Deserted! Jove!
And canst thou wink at this! I've treated them[8]
As brothers. The meanest in the ranks has shared
My crust. I fed as coarsely, slept as hard 25
As they. Partook their toils and led the way
In dangers. Yet deserted! Can it be!

SULPITIUS They are already at the city gates,
And greybeard senators, grown bold again,
Have set to work to find out all our worth; 30
And doubtless will decide we are too good
For Rome, and banish us.

MARIUS   Then discord reign and rage.
Let freedom be proclaim'd to all the slaves
Who join my standard. Slaves may surely fight

---

[5] Sulpitius had a law passed giving Marius the command of the campaign against Mithridates, and Marius had sent two tribunes to Sylla demanding that the army be turned over to them. "But Sylla, instead of resigning his charge, animated his troops to revenge, and led them, to the number of thirty thousand foot and five thousand horse, directly against Rome. As for the tribunes whom Marius had sent to demand the army of Sylla, they fell upon them and cut them to pieces." *Plutarch's Lives*, II, 270.

[6] On facing page: *ready Shouts, Drum and Trumpet, Red Fire and Lights.*

[7] L.20, interpolated above this line in another hand in pencil: "I learn from some undoubted source"

[8] Ll.23 through 27 cut in pencil.

For Freedom, when freemen sink to slaves.[9]   *35*

SULPITIUS   What means that glare of light?

MARIUS   Where?

SULPITIUS   To the west.

MARIUS   The dying glory of the setting sun.

SULPITIUS   He sets in clouds then[10] —see that wreath of
smoke!
Great Jove, the town's on fire. Here comes your
son.

Enter Granius[11]

GRANIUS   Arm, arm, my father.

MARIUS   Why this fearful haste?   *40*

GRANIUS   Sylla is in the city with his slaves;
They've fired the town to keep the citizens
Employ'd—Our friends in vain oppose their
march;
The streets are running blood and fill'd with
slain.

MARIUS   I'll be among them soon.

SULPITIUS   Lead on, lead on.   *45*
My anti-senate shall hew out your path.[12]

MARIUS   Alas! Sulpitius, 'tis a fearful hour[13]
And cannot end in good. When brothers raise

---

[9]L.35, canceled reading: " ... when freemen are willing to
become slaves./ See our forces marshall'd"

[10]In text and on facing page: *Storm ready Red Fire Drums
Trumpets Thunder and lightening, Alarms Lamps down*

[11][Left entrance]

[12]Ll.46 through 53 cut in pencil.

[13]Sylla led his army against Rome, and Marius killed many of
Sylla's friends. He offered freedom to slaves that would fight for
him, but Plutarch says only three accepted (*cf. Plutarch's Lives,*
II, 270); left with inadequate forces, Marius was forced to flee
and Sylla entered the city.

Th' avengeful sword against each other's throats
At ev'ry wound their mother country bleeds,   *50*
And though she prove the victor in the end
Her laurels must be steep'd in tears and blood.

SULPITIUS   In tears and blood then let us steep her laurels.

MARIUS   It is for life and liberty we draw;
And if the bright-eyed goddess now expire,   *55*
Her sacrifice shall be ten thousand hearts:
Her funeral pyre, the mistress of the world.

exeunt[14]

SCENE 3

The Forum. Night. Alarm without. A storm.[1]
Enter Cinna and citizens.

CINNA   What a night is this, my masters. The elements
are at war, and the thunder that roars above is
nearly drown'd by the shouts of the soldiers and
the groans of the dying.[2] The lightnings vivid
flash is scarcely seen by reason of the light that   *5*
issues from your burning homes, and the rain
falls less plenteously than the life's blood of our
citizens.

1ST CITIZEN   It is an awful night.[3]

2ND CITIZEN   What a peal was there.

1ST CITIZEN   Rome will be buried in ashes, and by tomorrow   *10*
Scarcely a child be left to mourn her loss.

CINNA   And this is done, my masters, to swell the
Pride of Marius, already grown too large

[14]*Shouts L H*
[1]*Lightning and Rain   Drums   Trumpets* On facing page: *Lights down*
[2]*Lightning*
[3]On facing page: *Thunder Loud*

To be confined within the walls of Rome.[4]

1ST CITIZEN   Down with him!

2ND CITIZEN   Kill—slay.

3RD CITIZEN   No Marius.   *15*

CINNA   Here comes Antonius to proclaim to you the
decree of the senate.

*Enter Antonius, preceded by lictors.[5]   He
ascends the forum.*

ANTONIUS   Draw near, ye men of Rome, and hear
pronounced
The judgment of the senate. Marius,
Whose boundless thirst for power has cost the
world
So many lives, his son, and that base slave,   *20*
Abhorr'd Sulpitius, now are doom'd to exile:
Denied the use of water and of fire—
A price set on their heads, and if they're ta'en
Within the Roman rule, it is decreed
That death's their portion—Death, immediate
death.   *25*
So flourish peace and liberty in Rome.   *descends*

1ST CITIZEN   Liberty, liberty!

2ND CITIZEN   Slay the traitors!

3RD CITIZEN   No Marius—No Marius! *exeunt.*

Enter Marius held by Sulpitius and Granius.[6]

---

[4]Historically, Cinna was a supporter of Marius. As the patrician leader of the democratic party, he deposed Sylla and urged
the recall of Marius who had fled to Africa. Marius returned with
a force of Italians and with the help of Cinna massacred Sylla's
friends in Rome.

[5][There are to be six lictors, entering from the right.]

[6][Right exit, and shouts in the background, and Marius to
enter from the right.]

MARIUS Off, off, unhand me, cowards slaves, and dogs—
Why drag me from the scene of carnage—off
And let me clothe me in the gory robe   30
Of liberty and death.

SULPITIUS   What, are you mad?

MARIUS Not yet, not yet, but ye will make me so.[7]
Hark how the tempest howls—
                                        Again! Again!
A sea of blood is flowing and I here[8]
Who should be boldly buffeting the waves   35
And swimming and rejoicing in their rage.

SULPITIUS Sinking, not swimming.

MARIUS   Sinking be it then!
I ask not for a death more glorious
Than thus incarnadined to meet the gods,
And firmly grasp the red right hand of Mars   40
With one as strong and bloody[9] as his own.

GRANIUS Be pacified—we struggle, sir, in vain.

MARIUS What says my son?

GRANIUS   Our friends are routed—slain—
And we must fly for safety.[10]

MARIUS   But the people?

SULPITIUS They have deserted you.   45
Intimidated by the approaching foe
They thought it prudent to desert their friends.

MARIUS The soldiers and the people both turn'd traitors!
Is there no act can touch the heart of man
With gratitude! I have stood forth for liberty;   50
Upheld the people and maintain'd their rights,

---

[7] *Shouts*
[8] Ll.34 through 41 cut in pencil.
[9] Canceled reading: "gory"
[10] On facing page, *Ready Shouts*

E'en when oppression brought her weightiest
   load[11]
To crush my dauntless efforts—I bore all!—
Nor had harsh threats, great promises and bribes
The power to make me falter. And behold,   *55*
They now surrender to the butcher's knife
The throat that oft grew hoarse in pleading for
   them.

   Enter Martha[12]

MARTHA   I sought for thee where death was revelling;
Yet my heart fail'd not, well assur'd that we
Should meet again.

MARIUS   Right. I would have it thus.— *60*
We should not part as passing strangers part,
Without a single sigh or a farewell.

MARTHA   But wherefore talk of parting?[13]

MARIUS   There's thy answer.—
You hear the storm approaching.

MARTHA   Let it come.
Mine has not been, you know, a life of sunshine *65*
Nor yet has thine. Remember thy own words—
"We've launch'd our barque upon a stormy sea,
Yet sail together, and there's much in that."

MARIUS   My actions are forgot; my words remember'd.[14]

MARTHA   Thy kind ones, ever.

MARIUS   And my harsh ones? *70*

MARTHA   I have not heard them yet, altho' 'tis said
That thou art harsh to all the world save me.

---

[11] Ll.52,53 canceled in pencil.
[12] [Martha to enter from the right]
[13] *Shouts*
[14] Ll.69 through 72 cut in pencil.

MARIUS   O! thou art still, e'en as the tender vine
That clings unto the oak. The ruthless storm
Has now uprooted it. Take heed, take heed,   *75*
Or it will crush thee in its fall.

MARTHA   But still
It is the nature of the vine to cling
Unto the prostrate oak, although it crush it.—

MARIUS   Go to thy rosy bowers—go—go and leave me.

MARTHA   'Twas in a storm more fearful far than this   *80*
That first we met: you bore me safely through—
I cannot leave you now; if we must part,
I'll leave you when the sun breaks forth again.

MARIUS   But will it e'er break forth again. I fear
My sun has set forever.   *85*

MARTHA   If[15] thou remain but true unto thyself
My prophecy must be fulfill'd.[16]

MARIUS   Enthusiast!
You know not yet the worst.

MARTHA   The worst is known.
E'en now as I pass'd by the capitol,
I heard thy banishment proclaim'd.

MARIUS   Ha banished![17]   *90*

MARTHA   Thee and thy son, Sulpitius and thy friends
And a reward is offered for your heads.

MARIUS   Banish'd and driven forth as if I were
The common enemy of man!

SULPITIUS   Quick work.
I wonder much what price Rome offers for   *95*
This head, she once thought worthless.

---

[15] Canceled; in another hand: "Do"

[16] The author attributes to Martha the prophecy made to the parents of Marius that he should seven times attain to the highest office. *Cf.* Act. I, Scene 3, n. 6.

[17] On facing page, *Drums and Trumpets R H*

MARIUS   Draw near, young hero, kneel and thank the
      Gods
      For crowning thus the promise of your[18] youth.
      And swear to consecrate your life and sword
      Unto thy country's freedom. Kneel, boy kneel.   *100*

GRANIUS   Nay this is mockery.[19]

MARIUS   And so it is.
      Then kneel and swear by all the destinies;
      By all the furies and the fiends that wait
      About the throne of hell, we'll not[20] forget
      The gratitude of Rome.   *105*

      Granius kneels[21]

MARIUS   Swear not to leave of all her guilty towers
      One stone unmov'd. Let not her temples nor
      Her gods escape the general scathe and ruin.
      Let neither age nor sex awaken mercy;
      But slay the husband in the wife's embrace;   *110*
      The trembling daughter clinging to her sire.
      And e'en the infant at the mother's breast,
      As ye[22] wouldst crush the Hydra[23] in the egg.

GRANIUS   I swear!

      Thunder[24]

MARIUS   Hark to that peal; the oath is register'd!   *115*
      And Mars, himself, has with his glove of blood
      Engrav'd it on his adamantine shield.[25]

[18] Canceled; in pencil in another hand: "thy"

[19] On facing page, *Red fire ready   Thunder ready*

[20] "we'll not" canceled; in another hand in pencil: "ne'er to"

[21] Cancelations and rewrite are unreadable.

[22] L.113 "ye" canceled; in another hand: "thou"; "the egg" canceled; in another hand: "its birth"

[23] The mythical offspring of Typhon and Echidna, in the form of a poisonous water snake that lived in the marshes of Lerna. The destruction of this serpent was the second Labor of Hercules.

[24] On facing page: *Loud Thunder*

[25] On facing page: *Red Fire*

Now let us hence. The night is dark, but lo!
The blazing towers send forth sufficient light
To guide us on our way. Hang on my arm.[26]   *120*
Thou little trembler—yet you do not tremble.

MARTHA   And wherefore should I, since I'm still with thee.

MARIUS   Bless you!
Rome, Rome, farewell! The time may come when we
Shall meet again. I loved you once, but now   *125*
Revenge shall be unto my sicken'd soul
As was in days of old, the hellish broth
Medea pour'd into the veins of Aeson.[27]
I rise regenerate—Anteus like;[28]
And though they heap a slavish world upon
        me[29]   *130*
It shall not make me groan, much less shall crush
        me.

        exeunt

[26]Ll.120-123 canceled and changed in another hand, to read:
"To guide us on our way./ Come thou foolish trembler./ And
wherefore tremble, since I'm still with thee."

[27]In the mythical story of the Argonauts, Medea avenged the
theft by Pelias of the throne of Iolcos in Thessaly from Aeson
his half-brother by restoring Aeson to youth by boiling him in a
cauldron of magic herbs. Pelias was urged to undergo the same
experience, but Medea used other ingredients and killed Pelias.

[28]A giant with whom Hercules wrestled. Whenever he fell, he
rose stronger than ever by contact with his mother, the Earth.

[29]On facing page, in various hands: *Fire Shouts Marius
changes dress*

ACT IV

SCENE 1

A street in Rome. Enter Sylla and Antonius.[1]

SYLLA   Thanks to the Gods that Rome is fairly freed
         From that distemper'd man, whose mad disease,
         Has been imparted to the public mind
         And rages like the plague, incurable.

ANTONIUS   What tidings have you of him?   5

SYLLA   He put to sea at Ostia, nearly famish'd,
         Deserted and alone; having escap'd
         By miracle the numbers who pursued him.[2]

ANTONIUS   Which course steer'd he?

SYLLA   Along the coast of Italy.
         The soil his dauntless valour once preserved   10
         From barbarous invasion. It is said
         He hoped to find a refuge in Minturno—
         Further I have not heard.

ANTONIUS   Let fate pursue him
         Until disgrace obliterate his glory!
         The senate has assembled to recall,   15
         Banish'd Metellus from his painful exile.
         Do you, my lord, direct your steps that way?

SYLLA   I would be present while an act is done
         So grateful to the feelings of all Rome.

         exeunt[3]

---

[1] [Sylla and Antonius to enter from the left]

[2] According to Plutarch, after Marius fled Rome as Sylla entered with the legions which he had refused to turn over to Marius for the Mithridatic campaign, Marius escaped by ship from Ostia, seaport of Rome, accompanied only by Granius, erroneously identified by Plutarch as the stepson of Marius.

[3] [right exit]

SCENE 2

The sea coast. A vessel at a distance. Enter Marius.[1]

MARIUS

The world conspires my fall; the elements
Take part against me; the ocean in affright
Repels me from her bosom, and the earth
Trembling beneath my tread denies a refuge.
Unparalleled reverse must expiate[2]   5
My proud success of life, and teach mankind
To admire my fall as they admir'd my fortune.
Then death come on, I'll here await my fate.[3]
'Tis not the first time, front to front we've
   scowl'd,
And I would brook thy fiercest look, and smile,   10
Even while[4] it froze the fountain of my life.
Ha! Sylla, thou would play the demi-god—
Sole ruler of an undivided world!
And my despair but seconds his ambition!
Gods! is it thus that Marius treats his foes!   15
Their best friends could not better serve them.
   But no!
Let cowards skulk to death. I'll still live on.[5]
Live and endure until the haughty few
Have ceased to lord it o'er their prostrate race,
And, disenthrall'd, man breathes a freer air.   20
Live on, until thy cursed senate, Rome,
Shall at my feet revoke its foul decrees,
And beg that mercy it denied to me.
Yes live, until for its last victory,

---

[1] [right entrance]
[2] Ll.5 through 15 cut in pencil.
[3] Ll.8 through 16 cut in ink.
[4] Canceled reading for "Ev'n while": "Though it"
[5] L.17, altered in another hand in pencil to read: "But no, cowards may skulk to death. I will live on." For the first sentence in this line, on facing page in pencil in another hand, an alternative reading: "But yet despite fates frown"

This arm has dragg'd thee, Sylla, to the dust   *25*
And held thee to the scorn of those who worship.
Live on, for life has charms remaining still.[6]

Enter Martha[7]

MARTHA   My search is fruitless; I can find no food.

MARIUS   We'll not starve yet! The vulture has his prey—
The wild wolf makes the wilderness his garner,   *30*
And shall we[8] starve where birds and beasts
    would fatten?

MARTHA   O, fear not that. It is decreed that thou
Shalt rule in Rome again, in spite of man.

MARIUS   Not for myself, poor child, not for myself.
But 'tis for thee I feel! For tho' my woes   *35*
Were countless as the sands on which we tread,
My deep anxiety for thee, poor child,
Would leave no room for other sorrows here.

MARTHA   My frame is slender, but my heart is strong.

MARIUS   Still not so strong but that the world may break
    it.[9]
                                          40
That way the world works miracles.
    Look there;
Their sails flaunt gaily in the wind; their
    barque[10]
Rides buoyantly and the waves kiss its prow;
But it is freighted with a heavier curse
Than it can safely bear. The treacherous waves   *45*

---

[6] Alternative reading, in another hand in pencil, for "remaining still": "in deadly hatred"

[7] [Martha enters from the right] In Plutarch's historical account, Martha is mentioned only in the episode leading up to the battle of Aquae Sextiae where in 102 B.C. Marius in his fourth consulship destroyed the army of the Teutones. Obviously, the playwright required her presence until the tragic conclusion, for dramatic effect.

[8] Canceled reading for "shall we": "must I"

[9] *galley ship moves*

[10] Ll.42 through 46 cut in pencil.

Will show to them the mercy that they show'd
  to me.
O! reckless[11] villains, to desert me thus!
On a rude coast, amid mine enemies,[12]
Betray'd and left to starve.[13]

MARTHA   Methinks I see a cloud of dust ascending   *50*
Above the summit of yon distant hill.

MARIUS   My eyes grow dim and I can nothing see
But moats obscurely dancing in the sunbeams.

MARTHA   Look yet.

MARIUS   I see it now.

MARTHA   A troop of horse appears—
Away; conceal thyself, for death's at hand.   *55*

MARIUS   When death's abroad should Marius lay [*sic*]
  concealed!
'Tis then no time for shrinking!— Jove pour on!
Like a brave swimmer I will stem the flood
Nor yield 'till it o'erwhelms me.

MARTHA   Haste—away.—
The sound of footsteps—ah! we are too late   *60*

    Enter soldiers[14]

CENTURION   Stand or die.

MARIUS   Thou hast a valorous throat.—
A cohort marshall'd 'gainst old Marius![15]

---

[11] Canceled reading: "coward"

[12] In Plutarch's account, after fleeing from Ostia, Marius had several narrow escapes from his pursuers until he was abandoned by frightened sailors on the coast near Minturno. *Cf. Plutarch's Lives*, II, 270-72.

[13] A canceled phrase at the end of this line: "O treacherous slaves."

[14] [Centurion and soldiers to enter from left]

[15] *Cf. Plutarch's Lives*, II, 272. A general order had gone through Italy for the death of Marius, and Geminius, military leader in Terracino, a coastal town some twenty-five miles from Minturno, had sent out a search party of soldiers, some of

Come on, ye base degenerate hirelings, come.[16]
Brandish your weapons, raise your polish'd
   shields
And plant yourselves in formidable array,   *65*
To hew to earth a naked unarm'd man.
Why stand ye all aghast! what! do ye fear?
Are ye the men[17] who fought against the
   Cimbri.[18]
Yet have not courage left to raise your swords
Against your leader's breast? Where is your
   valor?   *70*

   First soldier advances toward him

Stand back. Come on not singly—with a rush
Torn from the sand,[19] I'll put to flight thy
   courage.
Stand back, I say; back, back! Ye know me all!
And by the Gods I swear, the first who dares
Pollute my body with his slavish hands,   *75*
Dies.[20]
Forward! I'll follow you. Base slaves, obey!
'Tis Marius speaks, who ne'er commanded
   twice—
Ay,[21] Marius, who led you on to glory,
Now follows you to shame. Lead on, lead on.   *80*

   exeunt[22]

---

whom, no doubt, had fought in campaigns with Marius. They
discovered him hiding in a bog; they pulled him out naked,
covered with dirt, and delivered him to the officials at Minturno.

[16] Ll.63,64 canceled in ink.

[17] Marius refers to his successful rout of the Cimbri, Germanic
invaders, in 101 B.C. during his fourth consulship.

[18] Ll.68 through 70 canceled in pencil.

[19] Alternate reading, in pencil in another hand: "beach"

[20] L.76 concluded in pencil in another hand: "You all have
known me, I command you still."

[21] Alternate reading: "Old"

[22] [left exit] At the foot of this page in the manuscript is a
line in pencil in another hand, perhaps to conclude the scene: "I
never followed: always led the van."

SCENE 3

The council house at Minturno. Enter Sylla. [1]

SYLLA
My foe is captured and it is decreed
By those who rule the province of Minturno,
That he shall die; and yet the task is hard
To find one who will take upon himself
The office of his executioner.   5
For Marius th' achievements of thy sword
Are still remember'd here. But if there be
A reckless villain to be bought with gold,
His price, however great, shall not exceed
The limits of my hate to buy one blow.   10

Enter Martha [2]

MARTHA
I'll learn his fate—yes, from their lips I'll learn it.
I cannot linger longer at their door
Awaiting their decree, the patient scoff,
Of ev'ry passer-by. Ha! Sylla here!
Then I despair indeed! My fears are such,   15
I've scarce sufficient courage left to ask
The sentence. [3]

SYLLA   Death to Marius! [4]

MARTHA   Ha! death!
Let virtue fly the Roman character
And gratitude become an empty sound;
But let not Italy disgrace her name
By sacrificing him who once preserved her!   20

---

[1] [Sylla enters from the right] Historically, Sylla was not in Minturno but was occupied with mending political fences at Rome after the banishment of Marius and continuing the war against Mithridates.

[2] [Martha enters from the left]

[3] L.17 first sentence concluded in another hand: "What is the fate of Marius?" A further cancellation would have L.17 read only: "the fate of Marius?"

[4] "to Marius" canceled in pencil.

SYLLA   The course of justice must not turn away
          Tho' heav'n itself should fall. It is decreed
          That Marius dies, and justice sanctions it.

MARTHA   Thy hate, not justice, but thy rancorous hate.
          Had thy voice been but half as loud to save   *25*
          As to destroy, the people would have borne
          This exiled man in triumph through the streets,
          And cursed the baseness of the Roman senate.

SYLLA   Why fall your sharp reproofs on me, good Sibyl,
          Since I make not the laws, nor yet enforce them.   *30*

MARTHA   What brought thee here from Rome? Thy rival's
            life!
          Like the gaunt wolf, that scents his wounded
            prey.
          Thou, open-mouth'd, hast follow'd on the trail,
          And howl'st to lap his blood. But I will thwart
            ye—
          For if there is a spark of virtue left   *35*
          In all Minturno, I will find it out
          And rouse it to a flame, whose boundless rage
          Will make ye tremble for this act of—justice.

               exit[5]

SYLLA   I must be speedy or I shall be foil'd.
          Already do the people in the streets   *40*
          Talk loudly of th' injustice Rome has done
          To him who saved them from the Teuton's
            sword;[6]
          And if I strike not soon their gratitude
          Will foil my purpose yet.

               Enter a Cimbrian[7]

                              You've come at last.

---

[5] [Martha exits left]

[6] Marius had successfully routed the Germanic invaders, the
Teutones and their allies, the Ambrones, in 102 B.C., before
conquering the Cimbri.

[7] [The Cimbrian enters from the left]

CIMBRIAN   As early as your message was received.   *45*
What would you have?

SYLLA   Thou art a Cimbrian;
A sad survivor of that warlike race
O'ercome by Marius.

CIMBRIAN   A Cimbrian once
But now a Roman slave.

SYLLA   Wouldst thou avenge
The tortur'd spirits of thy slaughter'd race   *50*
And give them rest?

CIMBRIAN   Would I!—Say on.

SYLLA   Thou hast a sword.—Ay, firmly grasp the hilt!—
The law demands a blow should now be struck—
Wilt thou obey the law?

CIMBRIAN   And must that blow
Fall on a Roman throat?

SYLLA   He is a Roman.   *55*

CIMBRIAN   Then your slave obeys.

SYLLA   The deed once done and rich rewards are thine.

CIMBRIAN   Had he as many necks as poets give
The fabled Hydra,[8] I would lop them all;
And tho' they sprang in countless numbers forth *60*
From ev'ry wound, I would not cease the work,
Until this arm fell sinewless beside me.
Your slave obeys—the law shall be fulfill'd.[9]

       exeunt

---

[8] A poisonous serpent whose destruction was the second assignment in the Labors of Hercules. The mythical creature had many heads, and as soon as one was cut off, others grew to replace it.

[9] At close of scene, in pencil in another hand: "Sylla. 'Then follow me.' "

SCENE 4

A prison. Marius discover'd.[1]

MARIUS Was I reserved, ye angry Gods for this![2]
To have my life discuss'd by shallow knaves,[3]
And see fate dwindle to an idiot's breath
As fickle as the wind, forever changing.[4]
If these same learned sages were but forced   5
To take, with their own hands, the wretched life
Their voices have condemn'd—It would be sport
To win it from a myriad[5] of such things
And make it worth possessing by the deed.

Enter Sylla, disguised, and the Cimbrian[6]

SYLLA Behold him there; now while he's lost in thought   10
Strike home. Give him not time to turn his eyes,
But strike and fly.

CIMBRIAN   This sword shall reach his heart
Unless his ribs should prove to be of iron.

SYLLA Be resolute. Strike home.

Exit Sylla

MARIUS   An armed man here
With ruffian on his front!—Thy errand's known.   15
Stand off.[7] —Darest thou kill Caius Marius!

CIMBRIAN Ha! Marius!

---

[1] On facing page and on text: *Lights down*
[2] Ll.1 through 9 cut in pencil.
[3] Canceled reading for ll.1-4: "The lion's caged; his nails have been torn out./ And they dare now approach him. Great Gods!/ Was I reserv'd to have my life or death/ Discuss'd by shallow knaves?"
[4] "forever changing" canceled.
[5] Canceled reading: "cohort"
[6] [right-hand entrance through door in flat]
[7] Canceled: in pencil in another hand: [Stand] "back."

MARIUS
Yes Cimbrian slave[8] in me behold the man
Who dash'd thy nation from the tribes of earth,
And fatten'd Italy with their best blood.[9]   *20*
Raise thy bent neck and fix thine eye on mine.
Behold the man a world could not subdue;
Wilt thou attempt him, singly, and alone?

CIMBRIAN
I crouch for mercy—spare my abject life.

Throws down his sword

MARIUS
'Tis not for him who cramm'd the jaws of death   *25*
With thousands[10] at one meal, to turn aside
And crush a worm that's writhing at his feet.
Begone[11] —thou thing of aspen leaves, begone.[12]

Exit Cimbrian[13]

The lion's caged; his nails have been torn out
And they dare now approach him in his den.   *30*
O, that he had more room; again were free,
Tho' weary, wounded, hunted to the death,
His voice would make the forest tremble still.[14]

Enter Sylla, disguised[15]

Another comes! What art thou?

---

[8] Alternative reading in pencil in another hand, above this phrase: "Look in my eyes"

[9] Alternative reading in pencil in another hand: [with] "thy nation's" [blood].

[10] Canceled reading: "myriads"

[11] Alternate reading: "Arise!"

[12] In the historical account, a Gaul or a Cimbrian was dispatched by the magistrates to a house where Marius was under guard. When the assassin entered the chamber, he was struck with terror by the commanding eye and voice of his victim, threw down his sword and fled, crying, "I cannot kill Marius." This episode changed public opinion, and Marius was led to the seacoast and set free. *Cf. Plutarch's Lives,* II, 273, 274.

[13] *D in F:* [exit through door in flat]

[14] On facing page: *Ready Drum and Trumpet Shouts of Citizens ready behind*

[15] [Sylla to enter through door in flat]

SYLLA	Ask thy fears.
MARIUS	My fears were ever dumb.
SYLLA	I'll give them tongues. *discloses himself.* *35*
MARIUS	Sylla! And come to play the part, no doubt, For which the Gods design'd him. This is well.
SYLLA	I come to close my long account with thee, In one brief moment, so prepare to die.
MARIUS	The wise man always is prepared to die. *40* If thou art thus prepared, come on.

Takes up the sword left by the Cimbrian.

SYLLA	Ha! armed!
MARIUS	Come on, if thou hast courage; add my death To thy long list of crimes. Strike, strike I say For public malice and for private hate.

Alarm without[16]

SYLLA	What noise is that!
MARIUS	Why dost thou falter now![17] *45* Old Rome, and all my little snarling foes Will glory in the deed; to see my life Which roused their fears and envy, basely closed By such an executioner. Come on.

Noise without. Shouts

SYLLA	Again! I must be brief.
	Without. Marius! Marius! *50*
MARIUS	They come to rescue. Who takes my life shall pay for its full value.

*Fight. Marius disarms Sylla, hurls him to the
ground and bestrides him. Citizens break into
the prison headed by Martha.*

[16]On facing page: *Drum Trumpet Shouts*
[17]Ll.45 through first sentence of l.50 cut in pencil.

MARTHA	Speed to the coast; a barque lies there in waiting.
MARIUS	There's virtue in the people, still, by Mars![18] I've said it oft; their rulers are to blame, *55* And not the people—they are honest still.
MARTHA	Speed to the coast.
MARIUS	For liberty, for life and liberty.

Scene closes.[19]   *Shouts*

SCENE 5[1]

The coast of Africa. Enter Martha and three sailors.

MARTHA	We've had a boisterous voyage from Italy, But we are now on solid earth again. Fall down and kiss the sand in thankfulness.
1ST SAILOR	Not in such haste. We may be obliged to take to[2] our barque before tomorrow, for there appears *5* to be no resting place for Marius, either on land or sea.
2ND SAILOR	Here on the coast of Africa he may remain in safety and unknown.
MARTHA	He was not born to such a destiny. *10* A cloud may dim the brightness of the sun, But still it will burst forth in all its glory.

---

[18] Ll.54 through first sentence of l.57 cut in ink.

[19] In pencil at foot of the page, locations of the actors: Marius, center rear; Sylla, center front; Martha, stage-right; citizens, stage-left.

[1] This entire scene canceled in pen and pencil.

[2] L.5 to end of scene, irregular in initial capitalization and meter.

1ST SAILOR   Poor man, his fate bears heavily on him. He has not
tasted food for two days, nor has he spoken.
I fear me, he has become a manhater.   *15*

MARTHA   Do not forsake him; fallen as he is,
He yet shall rule in Rome; 'tis thus decreed
By all the Gods, and man cannot avert it.
Protect him now and ye shall be rewarded.

         Enter Centurion

CENTURION   You are strangers to our coast!   *20*

MARTHA   We are—Poor voyagers from Italy, fatigued
And weary of our passage.

CENTURION   The barque that rides at anchor there is yours?

MARTHA   It is.

CENTURION   The banished Marius was seen to land from it.   *25*
Which way did he direct his steps?

MARTHA   Towards the ruins of yon fallen city.

CENTURION   Hold your barque in readiness. Farewell.

         Exit Centurion

MARTHA   Farewell, if that be all. Behold[3]
A strange barque, well mann'd, has anchored   *30*
Near the beach, and Roman soldiers
Have just landed from it.

---

[3]The composition in this speech is irregular in the manuscript. The lines have been broken to approximate in the five-stress line.

SCENE 6

The coast of Africa.[1] *Enter Granius and Sulpitius and soldiers.*

SULPITIUS   Nay bear your woes, sir, as becomes a Roman.

GRANIUS   As it befits my nature I must bear them.
Although a Roman I am still a man.

SULPITIUS   Where's your philosophy?

GRANIUS   Philosophy!
Can all the ethics that grave Zeno[2] taught;   5
The precepts, wise, that flow'd from Plato's
    tongue,
Assuage the pain proceeding from a sting
An insect may inflict? If not, why bring
Philosophy to heal the broken heart.

SULPITIUS   Despair not yet.   10

GRANIUS   There is no room to hope, Sulpitius, none!
Her father's hate is deadly to my race,
And e'en the powerful love he bears his child
Must fall before its fury. O! my friend!
Methinks there's some invisible spirit   15
That watches o'er the fate of parted lovers,
And by mysterious breathings in the air
Disturbs the cords of sympathy that bind
Inseparable hearts, when evil threatens.
If this be so, the grief that weighs me down   20
Must be prophetic of approaching ill.

---

[1] In the historical account, after sailing from Minturno, the ship was driven by the wind to the island of Aenaria (now Ischia, off the west coast of Campania), where Marius found his stepson Granius and friends with whom he sailed to Sicily, where they narrowly escaped capture. They went on to the island of Meninx (now Gerbi, off the coast of Africa), where Marius learned that young Marius had escaped to Africa, and they determined to follow him there.

[2] Greek founder of the Stoic philosophy.

SULPITIUS   Thou hast chang'd natures with thy father's
               Sibyl.
            Yield not to woes imagination paints:
            The actual wrongs we feel and tamely bear,[3]
            Should prove enough to rouse the brave to
               action.   *25*

MARTHA   And so they will.

SULPITIUS   The sibyl here! Thy father is at hand.
            Thou faithful creature what has been his fate,
            Since last we parted at the gates of Rome?

MARTHA   He put to sea at Ostia, and escaped   *30*
            But narrowly, the hands of his pursuers.
            The rugged sea, his woes and want of food,
            Conspir'd to make him ill. They anchor'd first
            Hard by the Lyris,[4] and persuaded him
            To go on shore, and 'neath the cooling shade   *35*
            Await the influx of the ebbing tide.
            He did so, and o'ercome by long fatigue
            He slept, and when he woke, he was alone;
            The faithless sailors had deserted him.

SULPITIUS   An ill wind fill their sails!   *40*

MARTHA   The steps of his pursuers soon were heard.
            Too bruis'd and weary to attempt escape
            He trusted to concealment, and plung'd in
            The marsh o' the Lyris, and lay buried there.

---

[3] The remainder of this scene cut in pencil. An inserted leaf in the manuscript picks up the following line and concludes the scene, in the author's hand:
"Should prove enough to rouse the brave to action.
Here to the coast of Africa we've traced
Thy exiled father's course.—Pursue the search,
For we have that t'impart will raise a fire
From dying embers, that may yet reduce
Ungrateful Rome to ashes. On, lead on.
              exeunt."

[4] The Liris, now the Garigliano River. This passage is the account from Plutarch. *Cf.* Act IV, Scene 2, n.15. The remainder of this scene recapitulates the action of Act IV, Scenes 2 through 4.

Ere long he was discover'd and dragg'd forth,[5]   *45*
And carried to the prisons of Minturno.

SULPITIUS   Is this their gratitude to him who saved
Them and their brats from abject slavery!

MARTHA   The council met, and with one voice decreed
That he must die. No Roman could be found   *50*
To do the work of executioner.

SULPITIUS   Of course no Roman could be found for such a
deed.

MARTHA   A sad survivor of the Cimbrian race,
That Marius overthrew, was fixed upon.
He arm'd and enter'd where the exile lay.   *55*
And as he drew his murd'rous weapon forth,
Resolv'd to plunge it in his victim's heart
The hero turn'd his godlike front, and cried,
As if he still were in the battle field,
Commanding myriads of such abject things—   *60*
"Darest thou kill Caius Marius!" Jove's bolt
Could not have paralysed the slave
More than those simple words; he crouched and
shook,
Threw down his steel and fled.

SULPITIUS   O! all ye Gods!
I would I had been there!

MARTHA   The people now   *65*
Assembled and resolv'd that he should live.
A crowd soon gather'd at the prison gates,
And rent the bars asunder; then they bore
The prisoner in triumph to the sea
Where shipping lay all ready to receive him.   *70*
When placed on board the flaunting sail was
spread,
Fill'd with the blessings of a grateful people.

[5] Canceled line between ll.45 and 46; "And seem'd a raging
lion in the toils"

SULPITIUS   There's virtue in the people, still, by Mars!
             I've said it oft; their rulers are to blame,
             And not the people—they are honest still.   *75*

GRANIUS   How bears he his misfortunes?

MARTHA   Heavily—
             His wrongs have steel'd his heart towards
             mankind.

SULPITIUS   We've travell'd far in search of him. Lead on—
             For we have that t'impart will raise a fire
             From dying embers, that may yet reduce,   *80*
             Ungrateful Rome to ashes. On; lead on.

             exeunt

SCENE 7

*The ruins of Carthage. Marius discovered sitting
on the prostrate pillar of a temple, in deep
thought.*[1]

MARIUS   Ye fallen temples; desolate[2] palaces;
             Ye crumbling[3] sepulchres of unknown dead,
             And gorgeous emblems of ephemeral pride,
             Once rais'd your heads to crown a nation's glory,
             Now prostrate lie to consummate that end!   *5*
             Your fate is mine! How vain a thing is man,
             And the brief part he plays upon this scene!
             Yes; he whose voice was yesterday potential;
             Whose smile was life; whose angry look was
                 death;
             Now strays deserted through these lonely streets,   *10*
             With scarce as much of vain authority,

[1]On facing page and duplicated at this point in the ms.: *Lights
½ Down.* In pencil, [Marius to stand center stage while he
delivers this soliloquy]
[2]Canceled reading: "prostrate"
[3]Canceled reading: "lofty"

As the poor snail that drags his[4] slimy way
O'er fallen colonnades and gilt pilasters.
His passage can be traced—and so shall mine!
O! man, I hate thee and had rather herd   *15*
With brutish beasts than hold communion with
    thee.[5]
Thou hast the serpent's double tongue and
    venom;
The tiger's fierceness with the spaniel's fawning;
The ape's low cunning and fantastic tricks;
Thou'rt prone to bear oppression as the mule,   *20*
Yet dare to kick the lion's teeth when dying.
All that is base and vile in other things,[6]
Maintains a grade superlative in thee!
O! for a curse to tell how deep my hate!
But as there is no heavier ban[7] in store,   *25*
I pray the Gods may never change thy nature!

Enter Centurion

CENTURION   Lo! there he sits!
I feel a sacred awe while in his presence,
And my voice fails me, but it must be done.
Another load must fall upon the fallen.   *30*
Ho! Caius Marius! He heeds me not,
But like the prostrate pillar where he sits
Remains immovable. Ho! Marius!

MARIUS   Who calls?

CENTURION   I come, sir, from the Praetor Sextilius.

MARIUS   Go on—nay, falter not[8] —   *35*
If there's a curse upon thy tongue, speak out;[9]
I ask not mercy from the hand of man.

[4] Canceled reading: "its"
[5] Ll.16 through 21 cut in ink.
[6] Ll.22,23 cut in pencil.
[7] Canceled reading: "curse"
[8] L.35 concluded in pencil in another land: "Speak out I say"
[9] Ll.36,37 canceled in ink.

CENTURION   Your barque was seen to touch upon this coast,
And as the Roman senate has denied
To you the use of water and of fire,   *40*
Sextilius as a faithful governor
Forbids you to set foot upon this province.

MARIUS   I made him what he is!

CENTURION   Your answer sir?

MARIUS   Pour on your wrath, ye angry gods, pour on,[10]
Make e'en the meanest creatures of your hands   *45*
Your ministers of vengeance—I'll bear all!
The power that I bestow'd is arm'd against me!
Virtue has fled the world! Ingratitude
Stalks forth triumphant with her hideous front
To fright us from our natures. Centurion;   *50*
We served together under Scipio;
Fought side by side before Numantia,
Where you received that wound upon your
    forehead.

CENTURION   I well remember; and you slew the man
Who else had ta'en my life.

MARIUS   You see me here! *55*

CENTURION   I do my duty as becomes a Roman.

MARIUS   Duty!—thy duty!—
There's not a virtue in the human heart
But may be cancell'd by that little word;
And when men do what fiends would startle at,   *60*
They lull their conscience with a sense of—duty.

CENTURION   What answer shall I bear Sextilius?

MARIUS   Go—Go and tell him
That thou hast seen the exiled Marius

---

[10]Ll.44 through 50, exclusive of "Centurion," l.50, cut in ink.

Sitting upon the ruins of[11] Carthage.[12]   *65*

Exit Centurion

*Marius remains in deep thought for some time,
then rises hastily[13]*

MARIUS   Oblivious Jove![14] where will my sufferings end!
Have I been cast upon this heartless world
With thine[15] own impress on me, but to bear
Relentless persecution—countless woes!
Why was I fashion'd after thy[16] own image?   *70*
It had been mercy to have made me—dog—
The basest reptile that pollutes the earth,
Whose life is spurn'd and trod out by the thing
That struts the tyrant here. I'd rather be
The meanest of your works, than that I am.   *75*
For then I might have blest my lowly nature,
But now despise and curse it.

*During the foregoing Martha enters and stands
near Marius*

Who art thou?

MARTHA   Am I so chang'd that you need question me?

---

[11]Interpolation in pencil to read: [of] "proud" [Carthage].

[12]Plutarch recognized this climactic scene in the history of
Marius when the conqueror of North Africa finds himself deserted and at the mercy of Sextilius, then Roman governor of
the province. Instead of pity, he finds the rigid response of
Roman authority turned against him. In the ruins of the city
demolished in 146 B.C. by Scipio under whom he had fought as
a youth, Marius now delivered his greatest line. *Plutarch's Lives,*
II, 274, 275: "Thus, in the happiest manner in the world, he
proposed the fate of that city and his own as warnings to the
praetor." The editors of this English edition of Plutarch were
constrained to add their own footnote, p. 274: "There is not,
perhaps, any thing nobler, or a greater proof of genius, than this
saying, in Marius' whole life."

[13]From this point, through L.77 cut in pencil.

[14]Canceled reading: "Ye angry Gods,"

[15]Canceled reading: "Jove's"

[16]Canceled reading: "your"

MARIUS If thou art kindred to the human race
     Begone. Such creatures I abjure. They are   *80*
     Not honest. Hence, you but disturb my mind.

MARTHA I will not weep! I'm not a child of tears,
     Or this would make me weep.

MARIUS   Why linger yet?

MARTHA No mother's love assuaged my infant griefs.
     No father's care watch'd o'er my growing years; *85*
     I knew no kindred, scarcely knew a friend.
     I was a stranger in a stranger world,
     When first we met, and since that blessed time
     O! thou hast been, far more—far more to me
     Than father, mother, kindred, could have been. *90*

MARIUS And for that service, all I ask of thee
     Is to be gone.

MARTHA   Most cheerfully, to death
     If that will do thee service.

MARIUS   Go to death
     'T will do thyself a service, if not me;
     For what has such a frail and foolish thing *95*
     To do with life?

MARTHA   Nought, if you wish me dead.

MARIUS No greater blessing could I ask for thee.
     Death is life's bright inheritance. Sleep, if no
      more.

MARTHA Then I shall soon be bless'd.

     Enter Sulpitius and Granius

GRANIUS   Behold him there.
     How changed his manly bearing in his exile! *100*
     Is this the mighty mind kept Rome in awe!
     Alas! my father, do you know me not?

MARIUS I know thee for a man,
     Who curlike bites the hand outstretch'd to save

	And licks the foot that spurns him. Hence—	
	begone.	*105*
	Assume the viper's shape, and thou art welcome.	

GRANIUS   You wrong my nature.

MARIUS   Hence you trouble me.[17]

GRANIUS   Nay, look more kindly on your exiled son
           Whose heart is bursting[18] to behold you thus.

MARIUS   My son! Art thou my son?

GRANIUS   Your dutiful and reverential son.   *110*

MARIUS   Then call upon the Gods to pour out all
           The vials of their wrath upon this head;
           Heap curse on curse until the mighty weight
           Press like Olympus[19] on me—
           Invoke their fires to sear these aged loins;   *115*
           Dry up my blood and rack my joints with pain,
           Until the tortures of Ixion's wheel,[20]
           Sink into fable by comparison.

GRANIUS   Forbid it, Jove! say, why should I do this?

MARIUS   Because I gave thee being, sent thee forth   *120*
           To drink of poison with thy fellow man.[21]

SULPITIUS Nay, sink not thus beneath thy weight of woe.
           I've told thee often, sir, Rome could not move,
           Without our leading strings, and I have proved
           As true an oracle as dwells in Delphos.   *125*

MARIUS   Then go to Delphos—what care I for Rome.

SULPITIUS The sun breaks forth again; awake, 'tis day,
           And we no longer grope our way through night.

[17]L.106 canceled in pencil.

[18]Alternative reading: "breaking"

[19]In Greek mythology, Atlas was punished for his part in the revolt of the Titans against the gods by being required to support the heavens on his shoulders.

[20]In Greek myth, for his crimes against Zeus and Hera, Ixion was bound in the underworld to a ceaselessly revolving wheel.

[21]On facing page, *Wind instruments up*

MARIUS	Would it were one eternal starless night!
	That I might sleep forever—and not dream.[22] *130*
SULPITIUS	The people in their wisdom chose as consuls
	The stiff-neck'd Cinna, and the meek Octavius,
	Who are composed of jarring elements
	And cannot mingle into harmony.[23]
MARIUS	Let discord then prevail; 'tis nought to me. *135*
SULPITIUS	I say it's all to thee. A strife for power
	Ensued, and Cinna soon was forced to fly
	With numbers of his partizans from Rome.
	The standard of rebellion mocks the wind,
	And thousands, discontented, flock around it. *140*
MARIUS	It breaks upon me, great and glorious vision!
	The light's too great, it flashes through the brain
	Like Jove's all-searching fire.
SULPITIUS	Troops have been raised in Italy—
	Others await our orders in Numidia, *145*
	And Cinna knowing that your warlike skill
	Must prove resistless, asks your timely aid.
MARIUS	Go on, go on.
SULPITIUS	And as an earnest of his newborn friendship
	Confers on you the office of proconsul.[24] *150*

[22] Following L.130, in text in pencil, positions on stage indicated: Martha, stage-right; Marius right center; Sulpitius, left center; Granius, stage-left.

[23] Historically, young Marius found his father at Carthage and they escaped by boat to the island of Cercina, just off the African coast, just in time to avoid a pursuing troop of horse sent by Sextilius, the African governor. It was at this time that Marius learned of the contention at Rome between the consuls Cinna and Octavius, resulting in the temporary ascendancy of Octavius. Cinna, who had urged the recall of Marius, withdrew from Rome and gathered an Italian force to regain his power. It was this news that made Marius rejoice and determine to join Cinna. *Cf. Plutarch's Lives,* II, 275.

[24] According to the record, Marius landed in Tuscany where news of his arrival quickly brought to him a large force of assorted citizens from among whom he selected enough to fill forty

MARIUS   The storm has passed away; the clouds have
       vanished,
My burden's cast, and now I bound through
       ether,
Light as Minerva from the brain of Jove.
I see it now! I have it here, and here
Fast rooted!—closely intertwin'd with life: 155
They who would pluck it out, must pluck both
Heart and brain. Rest there and fester still!
That thought! Again! More light, more light,
       more light.
Ha! ha! ha!
O' that the human race had but one neck   160
My foot should soon be on it.

Enter soldier with fasces

GRANIUS   Here are the ensigns of your office, sir.

MARIUS   Take them away for pomp doth not become[25]
My ruined fortunes.

GRANIUS   Be persuaded, sir.

MARIUS   Take them away.

SULPITIUS   Do not despise these new-gain'd dignities.   165

MARIUS   I value not the mere parade of office
Since power consists not in gay robes and fasces.
Hence with that mock'ry—haughty Rome shall
       learn,
In humblest weeds I can fulfill my purpose.

Enter Centurion

What says Sextilius—what is his decree?   170

ships. He advised Cinna of his willingness to join him, and the
consul promptly accepted, sending to Marius the insignia of proconsul, an extension of military authority after the termination
of the one-year term of consulship. Marius rejected the honors,
preferring mean garb and a disheveled appearance as indicative of
his dejected condition.

[25] Ll.163 through 167 cut in pencil.

CENTURION   The senate's will must be obey'd, and you—

MARIUS   Must trust the waves more merciful than man.
Then be it so; I ask no other doom.
Our sails shall quickly wanton in the breeze,
And the glad waters dance around the prow;   175
While songs of triumph swelling o'er the sea,
Proclaim to Neptune on his emerald throne,
The exile's on his watery realm again:
And the arch'd sky as it returns the strain
Shall prove the measure of this hour is full.   180
Turn round the helm; prepare the lusty oar,
And steer for Rome, the mistress of the world.

  exeunt[26]

[26] At the end of the act: *Music Marius changes dress*

ACT V

SCENE 1

A street in Rome. Enter Metellus and Antonius.[1]

METELLUS   Despair is mark'd on ev'ry face. The streets
            Are throng'd with trembling citizens. All work
            Is now thrown by; all thoughts give place to
                fears.
            Our wives and daughters with dishevell'd hair
            Fly from their homes in terror. Household lars   5
            Are now neglected, while our earnest prayers
            Are offer'd up to Jove to intercede.

ANTONIUS   All things proclaim that Marius has arrived
            And storms[2] the gates of Rome to be admitted.
            What measures have been taken to appease him?   10

METELLUS   The senate has assembled and propose
            To throw the gates wide open, and thus let
            The famish'd wolf into the fold.

ANTONIUS   What greater curse could fall on hapless Rome!
            Is there no hope from Sylla?   15

METELLUS   Messengers have been sent to Capua,
            Where he is with the army[3] but I fear
            Our trembling senators will seal our fate
            Ere he arrive in Rome. Let us hence,
            And lend our aid t'avert th' impending ruin.   20

exeunt

[1] [right-hand entrance]
[2] Canceled reading: "knocks at"
[3] Ll.17 through 20 cut; in another hand: [with the army.] "Speak what news? *Enter a Citizen:* Our trembling senators have seal'd Rome's fate/ Urged by their coward fears they ope'd the gates/ And hail'd stern Marius as the seventh time consul."

SCENE 2

Cinna's camp.[1] Distant view of Rome. Marius discovered, alone, gazing towards the city.

MARIUS   I cannot turn my gaze from thee, fair city![2]
             How thy towers dazzle in the setting sun;[3]
             Thy domes and spires shine forth like burnish'd
                gold;
             And thou 'rt as joyous and more beautiful
             Than a young bride upon her bridal day!   5
             Still thou art doom'd. Tho' hills were set on hills
             And seas met seas to guard thee, I would
                through—
             And like a loving son beside thee stand,
             And watch thy parting throes.

             Enter Sulpitius and Martha[4]

SULPITIUS   Behold him there—(*to Martha*)
             Draw near.

MARTHA   It is in vain. Days have elapsed   10
             And he has neither deign'd to speak to me,
             Or even look at me.

MARIUS   Ha, what shrill pipe is that!
             There's music in that pipe, and passing sweet:—
             But notes like those belong not to a camp—   15
             At least to such a camp as this—as this!

SULPITIUS   There was a time when you were pleased to hear
             That voice in any place—It is your sibyl.

MARIUS   What say you, sir? O, I remember now.

SULPITIUS   Speak,—speak to him, before his mind resume   20
             Its wonted train of thought.

[1] *camp flats*
[2] On facing page: *Ready Trumpet R H*
[3] Ll.2,3 canceled in pencil.
[4] [left entrance]

MARIUS   O! Rome![5]

MARTHA   You're sad sir.

MARIUS   Never more merry—never.

MARTHA   Yet somewhat chang'd.

MARIUS   A little chang'd—Perhaps a little chang'd—
              Why do you sigh—all things are prone to change.

MARTHA   I once imagin'd sir, you ne'er would change   25
              Towards me.

MARIUS   And so did I—and so did I.[6]

SULPITIUS   You've not bestow'd a look of kindness, or
              A word upon her, since you sail'd from Carthage.

MARIUS   Indeed! I've been to blame. But there's my hand.
              The fault shall yet be mended—There's my hand.   30

              Martha takes his hand

SULPITIUS   His eyes still fixed on Rome!

              Martha bursts into tears and leaves him.

                                          Why do you weep?

MARTHA   'Twas as the freezing touch of one that's dead—
              His hand return'd not e'en the slightest pressure.

SULPITIUS   Retire. We'll seek some fitter time. Retire.

              Exit Martha[7]

MARIUS   I cannot take my eyes from thee, proud Rome!   35
              Thy walls, e'en now, were brazen battlements,[8]
              Then seem'd on fire, and then were lav'd in
                  blood.
              But now, methinks, an awful gloom hangs o'er
                  them;

              [5] Ll.21, second sentence through 26 cut in pencil.
              [6] On facing page: *Trumpet ready*
              [7] [left exit]
              [8] Ll.36 through 41 cut in pencil.

And lo! a flock of vultures from the west,
Descends upon thy towers! My own lov'd bird![9]   *40*
Sit there and croak—your festival is nigh.[10]

SULPITIUS   Behold your colleague comes.

MARIUS   Well, let him come.
He once pour'd all the venom of his tongue
Into my bleeding wounds; but strange reverse!
Now oil and balm to heal them. Let him come.   *45*

Enter Cinna followed by a soldier[11]

CINNA   Ambassadors from Rome! My friend and
colleague,
Shall we hear their suit?

MARIUS   Whose suit?

CINNA   The ambassadors from Rome.

MARIUS   They must be heard, or we offend the senate.

CINNA   Then give them entrance. *exit soldier*   *50*
In what solemn state
And idle pomp they move!

MARIUS   Man is ambitious of parade and pomp
Whether he mounts a scaffold or a throne.

Enter Antonius and two others[12]

ANTONIUS   To thee most mighty Cinna, and to thee,   *55*
Most injur'd Marius, in Rome's name
We bend the suppliant knee.

CINNA   What's your demand?

---

[9] According to Alexander of Myndos, two vultures, which had
been fitted with brazen collars by the soldiers and then released,
always followed the army of Marius before a successful battle.
Cf. Plutarch's Lives, II, 254.

[10] On facing page: *Trumpet R H*

[11] [right entrance and Granius to come with them]

[12] [right entrance, and senators and soldiers to accompany
Antonius]

ANTONIUS   Whither, O! whither will your rage pursue us?
             Must all the fortunes and the lives of Rome,
             Suffer for one miscarriage of her masters?   *60*
             Your sorrowful, afflicted mother Rome,
             In whose kind bosom you were nurs'd and bred,
             Stretches her trembling arms t' implore your
               pity.

MARIUS   If she's prepar'd to take us to her bosom,
             She'll find us, sons, worthy of such a mother.   *65*

ANTONIUS   Fold up your dreadful ensigns, and lay by
             Your warlike terrors, that affright her matrons,
             And come to her ere sorrow quite o'erwhelm
               her;
             But come like sons that bring their parents joy;
             Enter her gates with dove-like peace before ye   *70*
             And let no bloody slaughter stain her streets.[13]

MARIUS   I am a banish'd man and may not enter,
             Until the senate has revoked my sentence.[14]

CINNA   And is it thus you think to heal our wounds;
             Curlike to lick them well with flattering
               tongues?   *75*
             Go tell them to throw open wide their gates,
             Before our engines fairly test their strength.
             And tell them, farther, if they treat with me
             It is as consul. If you have that power,
             Say on—I'll hear you.   *80*

ANTONIUS   As consul, Rome is ready to receive you.

----

[13]On facing page: *Ready Flourish R H*

[14]Historically, Octavius, the upright consul in Rome, trusting
to omens, did not make proper defence for the city, and many
of the troops went over to Cinna and Marius. Octavius was slain
and the senate asked Cinna and Marius to come into the city, but
to spare the populace. Marius dissembled, saying he could not
enter until the senate repealed his sentence of exile. When the
people assembled for that purpose, Marius and Cinna began the
massacre that lasted for many days. *Cf. Plutarch's Lives,* II, 276,
277.

But on that brow there still appears a cloud
That never rose without a falling storm.

MARIUS   Alas! for me, a simple, banish'd man,
Expell'd [*sic*] my country by the right of law,   *85*
And justly punish'd as my ills deserved,
Think not of me; whate'er are his resolves,
I shall obey. Think not of me.[15]

ANTONIUS   May all the gods reward you.

      Exeunt Antonius and suite

MARIUS   Pious soul!
He prays for me, and yet would cut my throat   *90*
For half a drachma.

SULPITIUS   Gratis if he dare.

MARIUS   How beats thy heart?

SULPITIUS   As if 't would burst my cuirass and I feel
As twenty years were taken from my back.
E'en my old sword now leaps upon my thigh,   *95*
And the tough scabbard scarcely can contain it.

MARIUS   Well, it shall need no scabbard.

CINNA   Sound a charge;
Draw out our guards and let the trumpets swell.
Until the trembling walls of Rome resound
That Marius is at hand. Sound, sound a charge.

      Flourish of trumpets and drums[16]   *100*

MARIUS   Silence those stirring notes. They fill my mind
With thoughts of carnage. Change your stops, I
     say
To some more lively measure—such a one
As laughing Bacchus loves, when he performs
His saturnalia. Fill my mind with joy,   *105*
I go to meet my mother. Play on; play on.

[15] On facing page: *Ready Wind Instruments*
[16] On facing page: *Flourish*

SULPITIUS   What measures shall they strike?

MARIUS   I care not what,[17]
So it be light and soothing—Note a charge!
All things are joyous now. Play such a strain
As Orpheus breath'd in the Cinconean woods,[18]   110
And woke to joy e'en things inanimate.
Or such a one as Ericina pour'd[19]
When her soul melted for Adonis dead;[20]
I care not what, so it be light and soothing[21]
And make not discord in my well-tun'd mind.   115

         Music and exeunt[22]

SCENE 3

         The Forum. Enter Metellus[1]

METELLUS   Most shameful weakness, to betray our lives!
Were not our walls well mann'd, and Sylla too
At Capua, almost within a trumpet's call?
And to submit! shame to the senate—shame.

         Citizens cross stage

[17]Ll.107 second sentence, 108, canceled in ink through "soothing."

[18]Orpheus, the mythical sweet singer and purported founder of the Orphic religion, supposedly came from Thrace, where one of the earliest tribes were the Cicones—hence the "Ciconean wood."

[19]Ll.112,113 canceled in ink.

[20]A reference to the grief of Aphrodite, Greek goddess of love, when the youth Adonis was killed. Aphrodite, or the Roman Venus, had a sanctuary on Mt. Eryx in Sicily, especially honored by the Romans, hence the title "Venus Erycina."

[21]Canceled reading: "or sad"

[22]On facing page: *wind instruments;* also, [right-hand exit]

[1][right-hand entrance] The entire line is then canceled in ink, indicating that Metellus is on stage when the scene opens. Historically, Metellus never returned to Rome after his exile, but his son, Metellus, was in temporary league with Octavius, the consul who abandoned the city to Marius and Cinna.

CITIZEN	Already reeking murders in the streets; *5*
	Matrons with infants in their arms are butcher'd
	And Rome appears one noisome house of
	slaughter.
ANTONIUS	Whither, O!² Whither shall we fly for safety?
METELLUS	Even to our altars—³
	And if the Gods forsake us⁴ in th' extreme, *10*
	Then by the hands of one another die
	As Romans ought. Hark to that strain! they
	come.

*Music without*⁵

As if it were in mockery of death,
They drown the shriek of horror and despair
In light and joyous strains. Away! They come.   *15*

*exeunt*⁶

SCENE 4¹

The Forum. Enter Marius, Martha, Cinna, Gran-
ius, lictors and guards. Marius mounts the tribu-
nal. Music

MARIUS	I thank ye, Gods, ye have restor'd me now.
MARTHA *(appears in the crowd)*	Hail, Marius, hail!
MARIUS	Whose voice is that?

---

²"Whither, O!" canceled in ink.

³Canceled reading: "Ruin draws near us fast; fly to your altars."

⁴Canceled reading: "you"

⁵On facing page: *Wind instruments*

⁶[right-hand exit]

¹This is renumbered as scene 2, indicating that Forrest may have omitted Scenes 2 and 3.

MARTHA   All hail! I greet thee now,
          The seventh time consul of degenerate Rome.

MARIUS   My own true prophetess! Thou shalt be sent   *5*
          To Delphos. Thy skill is matchless sure!
          And Phythonissa [*sic*]² blind compar'd to thee.

MARTHA   I've lived to see my prophecy fulfill'd.

MARIUS   I would not ask thee to predict one hour
          Beyond the present. What's to come, is plain: *10*
          I hold the fates themselves within this hand.
          More music there! And be it so heavenly soft³
          It may not wake e'en Mercy from her slumbers.

          Enter Sulpitius with a head which he presents
          to Marius

MARIUS   Whose head is that?

SULPITIUS I found it on the shoulders of Antonius,⁴ the
              orator;   *15*
          But now 'tis thine.

MARIUS   His eloquent tongue is mute; it shall no more
          Be prostituted to support oppression,
          And wrong the weak. The poor man's right
          Though guarded by the seven-fold shield of
              justice   *20*
          Shall cease to dwindle 'neath the weight of
              words
          And windy argument. That tongue is mute
          Which stole men's hearts away in spite of reason,
          And made the blacker seem the whiter cause.

---

²The Pythia (Pythonissa) was the inspired priestess at Delphi.
³Ll.12 through 32 cut in pencil.
⁴Historically, the hiding place of Antonius was divulged to
Marius, who sent an officer, Annius, with soldiers to kill him.
The soldiers were so moved by his eloquent pleas for mercy that
they stood and wept, but Annius rebuked their weakness and
himself cut off the orator's head. *Cf. Plutarch's Lives*, II, 278.

SULPITIUS   The soldiers who ascended to his room   *25*
With daggers drawn to sheathe in his old heart,
Gave ear unto his voice, and soon return'd,
Charm'd from their bloody purpose. I rush'd up,
And ere his lips had time to move, I smote him.

MARIUS   What said he dying?

SULPITIUS   He pleaded still for life,   *30*
And like the swan, his notes were musical.

MARIUS   He hated me and he has met his doom.

Enter soldiers with Metellus[5]

GRANIUS   Metellus has been found.

MARIUS   Metellus, ha!
A thousand talents for the glorious news—
Where is he? Bring him forth.

Enter Metellus and soldiers

METELLUS   He stands before you.   *35*

MARIUS   The core of my disease at length is found;
I soon shall tear it out and be at rest.

METELLUS   Thou tiger in the human form, what death
Must I endure? Begin; I am prepared.

MARIUS   I shall be merciful.

METELLUS   Thou merciful!   *40*
Yea, as the famish'd wolf. Thou merciful!
Behold our dwellings pillag'd and consum'd;
Our matrons fleeing from their ravishers;
Our children slaughter'd and the public streets,
O'er-flooded with the richest blood in Rome.   *45*

MARIUS   'Tis for the people's good such riches flow
Thus publickly.

---

[5] This line canceled; in pencil in another hand: "Enter R Granius" (Granius had entered with the other actors at the beginning of the scene.)

METELLUS   Thou taunting fiend! Cannot
This awful scene awaken pity in
Thy savage heart?

MARIUS   My heart! Speak not of that!
'Twas hunted from my bosom by the senate;   *50*
'Twas buried in the prisons of Minturno;
'Twas crush'd beneath the wreck of mighty
     Carthage!
Talk not of that.

METELLUS   Can nothing move thee?

MARIUS   Yes.

METELLUS   Speak; and to save my country, even I
Will bend the stubborn neck, and supplicate   *55*
Thy mercy. Speak.

MARIUS   Thy weak complaints may move me—to derision.

METELLUS   Hear him, ye men of Rome! Is this your choice?
Have ye become barbarians that ye choose
A savage for your ruler. See him there,   *60*
Insensible to all th' appeals of nature,
As the stain'd weapon he now firmly grasps.
Those lips that he now gnaws in fiendish rage
Were never parted but to breathe a curse
Upon mankind. That cold and haggard eye   *65*
Ne'er smiled with pleasure but on scenes of
     blood;
And Mercy never deign'd to shed a tear
Upon that iron visage.

MARIUS   Peace, old dotard.

METELLUS   Gods! Can it be, this is the peasant boy
I found among the cottages of Arpos;   *70*
Rear'd him to arms, and made him my
     lieutenant,
Which service he ungratefully return'd
By robbing me of office and of honor.[6]

---

[6] "and of honor" canceled.

MARIUS   Peace, I say.

METELLUS   Is this the man who once obtain'd a triumph   *75*
For service those more valorous had done!
Who stole the laurel from brave Sylla's brow
And blush'd not to entwine it round his own.[7]
And such a man, O! Romans, can ye choose
To rule the destiny of earth.

MARIUS *(hastily descends and stabs him)*   Die, die!   *80*

METELLUS   A nobler death I merited than this;
But any death is better than to live
In Rome.

MARIUS   Thou hast thy wish, then.   *A shriek*

METELLUS   Ha! that voice!

        Exit Granius[8]

        It is Metella's voice. My child,
And fleeing from a ruffian—Give me a sword—   *85*
It is a father's cause. Great Jove, I fall—
The hand of death is on me. *Falls*

MARIUS   Ha! ha! ha![9]

METELLUS   *A shriek*   Again! ye Gods, is there no father here?
O! spare my child and let me die in peace.   *90*
I ask but this. Ye will not drive me mad.

SULPITIUS[10]   Her life is saved. The ruffian writhes in death.[11]

METELLUS   Ah! who is he so merciful among you?

SULPITIUS   The son of Marius.

---

[7] A reference to Marius' assuming full credit for the conclusion of the Jugurthine war, when it was Sylla who actually accomplished the capture of Jugurtha.

[8] [Sulpitius and Granius exit left]

[9] Ll.88 through 91 cut in pencil.

[10] [Sulpitius to enter from the left]

[11] On facing page: *ready Wind Instruments*

METELLUS
                                        The gods reward him.
I've cursed his name thro' life, in death I bless it.   *95*
Marius, thy hand—I have scarce breath to say—
The brink o' the grave is no place for revenge—[12]
Thy country—spare thy country. *dies*

MARIUS
                                        He is dead!
My hand is stain'd with blood—the blood of him,
Who drew me from obscurity to light.   *100*
That thought—that thought—it must not take
  root here.
He should have died—by any other hand.
Remove his marred body from my sight,
And have his ashes decently inurn'd.[13]
Swell high your martial notes, and fill my soul   *105*
With thoughts more fitting to the times and me.
On to the capitol and there prepare
A festival. Ay, in the capitol!
All things in Rome are subject to my will,
And I will drink potations to the gods   *110*
E'en from the judgment seat of conquer'd
  worlds—
On to the capitol.

Scene closes[14]

SCENE 5

*A street. Enter Granius, supporting Metella,
wounded.*

GRANIUS
Lean on my arm, poor trembler; fear not now;
The slave is slain whose hands were rudely laid
Upon thy spotless form.

---

[12] L.97 canceled.

[13] On facing page: *Guards remove Met.*

[14] On facing page, in two hands: *March Bold,* and instructions
that instruments exit left, drum and trumpets, right.

METELLA   That voice—that gentle voice!
It sounds like music to the troubled mind
When madly bursting from a dream of horror.   *5*
Speak, speak—who art thou? Let me hear that
   voice.

GRANIUS   He who was born to be thy bane, Metella.[1]

METELLA   Ah! Granius! Can it be?

GRANIUS   The wretch you name.

METELLA   'Tis well; we meet as we should meet; If I
Was ever dear to thee, and I have cause   *10*
To think thy tenderest feeling dwell with me—
This meeting is well timed.

GRANIUS   What means my love?

METELLA   Look on this stain;[2] it is my life's blood,
   Granius.
The slave you slew had given me my death blow
Before you came to rescue. I am faint.   *15*
These jewels tempted his rapacious hands,
And as I struggled to get free he smote me.
Such are the soldiers Granius leads against
His country and his friends.

GRANIUS   Have I endur'd life's bitterest agonies   *20*
To meet with this at last?

METELLA   I will not now reproach,
Though thou hast been a fatal source of grief
And turn'd awry the current of her life
Who would most willingly have borne for thee   *25*
The sharpest sorrows fate could have impos'd—
Yet I will not reproach.

GRANIUS   Thy words are death.

METELLA   Thy desperate revenge has now recoil'd

---

[1] L.7 canceled except for "Metella."
[2] Canceled reading: "scarf"

	And smote thee to the earth, for well I know
	Fate could not find a surer way to reach thee, *30*
	Than through my life.

GRANIUS   It could not. O! Metella!

METELLA   Oh! Granius, I have suffer'd much for thee:[3]
I have not breath to tell what I have borne!
But nought could root thy image from my heart.
I'm faint—support me—O! I'm deadly sick.   *35*
      faints[4]

    *Enter soldiers with litter, bearing the body of
    Metellus.*

GRANIUS   She dies! she dies! Metella, O! Metella!
Look up and bless me with the cheering light
Of thine eyes once more. Do not leave me yet.
She stirs—she breathes again.

METELLA   Where am I? Ah!

GRANIUS   Safe in the arms of him who loves.

METELLA   But ah![5]   *40*
Those frightful men! What do they here? A
    corse![6]
There has been murder done. Whose corse is
    that?
His robe denotes him of Patrician rank.
What noble Roman has been butcher'd? Speak—
I charge you, speak.

GRANIUS   Nay loved one let them pass.   *45*

METELLA   Unhand me, Granius. Wherefore are they mute?
I must be satisfied. A frantic thought,
Comes rushing on my mind in mad array

---

[3] Ll.32 through 40 cut in pencil.
[4] On facing page: *Wind instruments ready;* in text, *solemn music.*
[5] *Pointing off*
[6] On facing page: *Ready Drums and Trumpet R H*

To fright me from my reason. Loose your hold.[7]
I will be satisfied. *Goes to the litter and
uncovers it.*

My father—O!   *50*

GRANIUS   Look down, ye gods, in pity on her woes.

METELLA   And is it thus with thee—cold, cold as stone!
'Tis well, 'tis well! How placidly he smiles.
I, too, can smile. That pang was to the heart—
Father beloved, receive thy dying child.   *55*
Upon thy clay cold bosom. *falls on the litter*

GRANIUS   *Raises her* She is dead!
The father and the child both dead! Ye men of
blood
Bear on your sacred burden—I will follow,
And pay that duty to these sad remains,
That from the living was too long withheld.[8]   *60*

*Exeunt. Granius bearing the body of Metella,
following the litter.*

SCENE 6

The capitol. A festive board decorated.[1] *Marius
and soldiers seated with goblets before them.
Martha the sybil near Marius. Cinna and Sulpitius
standing at the wing.*

MARIUS   Fill up your goblets till the rosy wine

[7]Ll.49 through end of scene cut in pencil. On facing page, in
pencil in another hand:
  "Metella—[To fright me from my reason] Oh heaven it is my
  father's corse. (She falls exhausted into the arms of Granius.)
Gra.—Look down ye Gods in pity on her woes.
Met.—That pang was to the heart
  Father beloved receive thy dying child.
  (She dies and is born off by Granius)"
[8]On facing page: *Wind Instruments slow;* in text, *Music slow*

[1]On facing page: *ready Trumpet R H;* in text: *Flourish*

Sparkle like Sylla's blood. Drink to the shades[2]
Of the Ambrones and the Cimbri; drink
To those whom Marius vanquish'd. See, they
   come:
The yelling spirits of the savage Teutons,   *5*
And mad Jugurtha foaming 'neath his chains,
Arise to join the pledge. Drink deep, I say
To th' enemies of Rome, for they are now
The friends of Marius.

SULPITIUS   How his eyes glare![3]

MARIUS   Who was it saved ungrateful Italy   *10*
When swarms of savages like locusts came,
To fatten on her fertile fields and vineyards?
Whose name struck terror through the countless
   horde
And check'd the progress of the sweeping deluge,
And turn'd its fearful course? 'Twas Marius!   *15*
Who was it led proud Afric's haughty king,
In triumph at his chariot wheels through Rome,
Until the monarch who for years defied her,
Became imbecile and deprived of reason?
'Twas Marius!

CINNA   Is this the far-famed soldier![4] *20*

MARIUS   Who was it fought for this rebellious city;
Brought trophies to her temples; had red honors
Hewn on his body, 'till the name of Roman,
Became a passport through the humbled globe?
Still Marius! And yet he has been doom'd   *25*
To reap the harvest of ingratitude
For all his services.

CINNA   Alas! vain boaster.

---

[2] L.2, "Drink to the shades" through l.7, "Arise to join the pledge." cut in pencil.

[3] Ll.9, second sentence, through 20, " 'Twas Marius!" cut in ink, but in margin, "restore this"

[4] Ll.20 through 27 cut in pencil.

Enter Granius[5]

MARIUS   How now, my son! So pallid, woebegone,
Thou lookest like a tenant of the grave.

GRANIUS   I would I were. I have just left the dead.[6]

MARIUS   True, death rides forth in purple[7] glory now—   *30*
His chariot wheels run axle deep in blood.
What bring you, boy, what news?

GRANIUS   Sylla with all his forces is before
The city walls.[8]

MARIUS   So soon!

SULPITIUS   He changes color,[9]
And at the name of Sylla his whole frame shook.   *35*
   Aside.

MARIUS   More wine. An icy chillness creeps around my
   heart.
Th' infirmities of age are coming o'er me.
Wine, wine, I say, to melt the ice within.
How stand our forces?

GRANIUS   Lost in mad excess.

MARIUS   Ha! ha! ha! They live like devils but they'll
   die like Gods!   *40*
Pledge me a cup to Mars, who stood my friend
In times of greater peril than the present.
My brain's on fire. Ha! See another comes![10]

---

[5] [right-hand entrance]

[6] Ll.29 through 32 cut in pencil.

[7] Canceled reading: [in] "all his" [glory].

[8] Historically, Cinna finally put an end to the carnage in Rome. Marius was chosen consul for the seventh time, but the news that Sylla was winning victories in the East and disorders caused by his hardships brought about the death of Marius within the first month of 86 B.C. almost four years before Sylla returned to Rome. *Cf. Plutarch's Lives,* II, 279, 280.

[9] Ll.34, "He changes color," through 39 cut in pencil.

[10] On facing page: *Trumpet R H*

Enter Centurion[11]

My army's made of shadows, and will startle[12]
If a breeze blow rudely. There was a time[13]   45
When Roman soldier was a fearful name!
O! where are ye who battled by my side
In Africa! Men now are made of fears
And blanch and tremble if a foe but frown.
Speak out thy errand if thy faltering tongue   50
Retain its functions still. Speak, speak, I say.

CENTURION[14]   A parley has been sounded and the foe
Demands the city gates to be thrown open.

MARIUS   Would ye betray your consul?

CENTURION   Now while I've life.

MARIUS   There spoke the old Roman virtue.   55
Had I a thousand faithful hearts like thine;
Weak as I am and sore oppress'd by fate[15]
Th' insolent foe should fly at my approach,
As timid lambs before the famish'd wolf,
But as it is—quick—hasten to your comrades,   60
Exhort them to defend their trust like Romans—
I am not what I was.

Exit Centurion[16]

SULPITIUS   His energies are gone.
Nature too long has been upon the stretch.

CINNA   What measures of defence do you propose?

MARIUS   Sulpitius, brave old heart; draw nigh—draw
nigh.[17]   65

[11]Canceled reading: "soldier"
[12]Canceled reading: "tremble"
[13]Ll.45 through 51, "Retain its functions still." cut in ink and
pencil; in margin: "restore this"
[14]Canceled reading: "Soldier"
[15]Canceled reading: "fortune"
[16]Canceled reading: "Soldier" and [exit right]
[17]Ll.65 through 76 cut in pencil; in margin: "Restore this"

Dost thou remember—but I'm sure thou dost—
How bravely once we strove to raise from earth,
The shackled figure of our grovelling race,
And thought to kindle to a sacred flame
Th' ethereal spark that Jove in mockery   *70*
Bestow'd on all.

SULPITIUS   Full well do I remember.

MARIUS   It was a joyful time!

SULPITIUS   It was indeed.

MARIUS   Art thou, of all the world, the only one
Hast not forgot. Can they forsake me now!

SULPITIUS   As they did once, 'tis like they will again.   *75*

MARIUS   And so it is. 'Tis strange that fact escaped me!
Bring all our forces to defend the walls,
And die or conquer; freedom is in both.

SULPITIUS   I'll conquer, or this parting is our last.

               Exit with Cinna[18]

MARIUS   I'll trust to Mars and here await the issue.   *80*
Where is my son—my persecuted son!

GRANIUS   Borne down with grief I stand before you, sir.

MARIUS   Thou'rt chang'd indeed. A strange and woeful
             change.[19]
This cannot be the work of adverse fortune!
Thy mind should soar above the things of earth.   *85*

GRANIUS   Metella's dead!

MARIUS   Poor girl! Poor innocent!
The storm that strikes the gnarled oak to earth
Spares not the blooming flower. Metella dead!
Her high born father, too, whose only fault
Was that his mind was suited for a god!   *90*

[18] On facing page: *Ready drum and shouts R H*
[19] Ll.83 through 98 cut in ink.

Look on this hand—'tis cover'd with his blood!
I've shed the lives of legions in my time;
The stream has flow'd as freely as the waves
That wash the banks of Tiber. Yea, it flow'd
And left no trace upon my memory.   *95*
Yet these few stains upon this palsied hand
Weigh like a mountain on me.

GRANIUS   Think not of them.

MARIUS   I shall not long; I feel I shall not long!
Come to my arms, thou tempest broken scion
Of a too rugged stock. We soon shall part.   *100*
I once imagin'd, that when dying, boy,
I should bequeath a glorious legacy
To him, upon whose front great Jove had
        stampt,
The scowl of Marius. A foolish wish!
And now though bankrupt and devoid of worth   *105*
I still bequeath the same.

GRANIUS   And what is that?

MARIUS   The world; 'tis thine, but 'tis not worth
        possessing.

MARTHA   I echo thee, and cry "not worth possessing!"[20]
But woe to man, adversity alone
Can fully teach its utter worthlessness.   *110*

MARIUS   My ever gentle sibyl, near me still!
As fond, devoted, as in happier days,
In spite of all my harshness. Bless thee, girl!
If but one tear were in this wither'd heart,
'Twould fall for thee.

MARTHA   And wherefore weep for me?   *115*

MARIUS   Death—death is near.

[20]On facing page, locations, in pencil in another hand:
Martha, stage-right; Marius, center; Granius, stage-left.

MARTHA He cannot come too soon.
I once imagin'd I was born to live,
But time has taught me I was born to die.

MARIUS So resolute! My own girl to the last!

MARTHA Thine to the last.[21]

Enter Cinna[22]

MARIUS What tidings now? *120*
But do not speak; I know it by thy looks!
I feel it in the chilling atmosphere
That now pervades thy presence; thou canst be
No other than the messenger of ill.

CINNA The gates are broken down and Sylla's forces *125*
Have now gain'd full possession of the city.[23]

MARIUS Stop, stop thy raven throat! More wine, more
wine![24]
This chillness steals upon me, yet my brain
Rages like Aetna. Fill up to the brim.

CINNA Our soldiers threw away their arms and fled, *130*
And thus became the easy victims of
Their conquerers.

MARIUS Silence ill-omen'd bird.
What means this trembling that invades my
frame!
It cannot be that Marius in his age
Has learnt to fear! I'm[25] cold as death. Wine,
wine! *135*
To fire the brain and warm the failing heart.

---

[21] On facing page: *Drum and Shouts R H*
[22] [right-hand entrance]
[23] On facing page: *Ready Crash R H*
[24] Ll.127 through 132, "Their conquerors." cut in pencil; in margin: "restore this"
[25] Canceled reading: " 'Tis"

Enter Sulpitius wounded and falls at the feet of Marius[26]

Ah! This looks well! There's blood upon thy
  brow.
A Roman soldier of the ancient stamp!
There has been fighting here.

SULPITIUS   The day is lost.

MARIUS   Who says it's lost while Marius commands![27]   *140*

CINNA   The foe approach; 'tis madness to remain,
And sheep-like here be slaughter'd, in the fold.[28]

MARIUS   Stand, stand, I say; I am your consul still.
Where is Sulpitius?

CINNA   Dying at your feet.   *145*

MARIUS   Then all is lost indeed!

SULPITIUS   I told thee I would either die or conquer;
I could not do the one—I'll do the other.

MARIUS   Thy words were ever "Liberty or death!"

SULPITIUS   I join them now, 'tis "Liberty *and* death."   *150*

               dies

MARIUS   My staunch old soldier dead! Metellus dead!
Antonius and the rest! Then what is life,
Since my revenge is glutted to the fill
And cannot rouse the ashes of the dead.[29]

GRANIUS   The outward gate is forced. Fly, fly, my father.   *155*

MARIUS   Marius never fled—but once.[30]

---

[26] On facing page: *Drums Shouts R H*

[27] *shouts*

[28] L.142, canceled reading: "and here be slaughtered, sheep-like in the fold."

[29] On facing page and in text: *Crash and flourish*

[30] After l.156, a canceled line: "Martha takes a goblet and empties poison into it."

GRANIUS   Fly from the power of Sylla.

MARIUS   The slave of Sylla!

MARTHA   Never shall a page so black as that
                Be found upon the records of the world.
                This potent poison shall confirm my words.   *160*

                She pours the poison in the goblet.

MARIUS   Never. What dost thou with that goblet in thy
                   hand?

MARTHA   I'll drink with thee, before we part, as we
                May never meet again.

MARIUS   And what's thy pledge?

MARTHA   I'll give thee—Freedom—freedom!

MARIUS   I'll pledge thee to the bottom of the cup;   *165*
                But let thy lips first sweeten it, my child—
                We've had too much of the bitter cup, already.

MARTHA   I drink to thee and freedom.   *drinks*

MARIUS   Here's to thee
                And freedom. Why dost thou smile?   *drinks*

MARTHA   'Tis done, and we are free!³¹

GRANIUS   Nay linger not; a minute lost, and we are lost
                   forever.   *170*

MARIUS   My limbs refuse their office, and my joints
                Grow stiff. I freeze.

GRANIUS   Help to support him hence.³²   *alarm*
                They come—they come.

MARIUS   The icy drops of death
                Are on my frame, and the hot blood of old
                Metellus burns like molten lead. See there!   *175*
                All stain'd with gore he writhes in agony,

---

³¹ On facing page and in text: *Shouts R H*
³² On facing page: *Flourish and Shouts R H;* in text: *shouts.*

And looks forgiveness on the wretch who slew
    him.
He stretches forth his hands imploring mercy!
The hands that foster'd me in early youth!
A cherub's smile is on his pallid lips,   *180*
But now distorted with the pangs of death!
Madness! Remove him from my sight! Away—
Take him away, I'll be a soldier yet.[33]

GRANIUS   Alas! my father![34]

MARIUS   I am sick to death—
Press thy poor father's hand.[35]

GRANIUS   'Tis cold as ice.   *185*

MARIUS   And trembles, too, my son.
O! what a pang was there! And yet another!
My bosom is too small—it heaves to bursting.
Feel how it throbs!—More air—more air!—I die!
Help me to rend these close-knit ribs asunder—   *190*
Help me! O! help!

      Martha falls

CINNA   Look to the Sibyl, there—

GRANIUS   Press not thus closely on him.

MARIUS   Soft. Bend me forward. So,—I breathe again.
My eyes grow dim. More air—more air.

CINNA   The Sibyl's dead!

MARIUS   Thou dear devoted one! *195*
Then the last human tie is rent in twain.[36]
The Gods have done their worst, for Sylla comes,
And I am breathing still. Death, death, where art
    thou?

[33] Following l.183: *Flourish*

[34] Ll.184 through 205 cut in ink and pencil.

[35] On facing page, there are illegible jottings in pencil; in text, contradictory directions, each canceled: "Sybil falls; restore this; out."

[36] *Shouts*

Enter Sylla and soldiers[37]

Stand off and touch me not till I am dead;
Avaunt, and let me die as I have lived,
Unshackled both in body and in mind.
Take him away, I'll be a soldier yet.   *200*
Ha! Sylla comes!

  *Sybil falls.   Flourish.   Enter Sylla and soldiers
  at back entrance.*

Let Rhadamanthus[38] then prepare his court
And pass his doom.   *205*

  Rushes forward to attack Sylla and falls

'Tis done; and Sylla now this world is thine;
But for me, freedom, freedom, freedom with the
  Gods.

  dies[39]

Sylla, 'tis past with me, and I bequeath[40]
An abject world to thy unpitying care.
Now unoppos'd, go drive thy chariot wheels[41]   *210*
Across the necks of slaves, who will not groan
Lest it offend the ears of Godlike Sylla—
But for me—Freedom, freedom, freedom
With the Gods!

  dies

THE END

---

[37]On facing page: *Soldiers on R and L;* in text: *Trumpets Drums*

[38]Mythical son of Zeus and Europa, a ruler and judge in either Elysium, the abode of the blessed, or of Tartarus, the place of the damned, where he is one of the judges of the dead.

[39]*Slow music*

[40]Ll.209 to the end are on the last page of the manuscript, an alternative ending to be picked up at 1.207. This alternate reading was the ending of the play as printed in the *Philadelphia Saturday News,* Jan. 7, 1836.

[41]Ll.210 through 213 canceled; in margin: "restore this"

Richard Penn Smith's Dramatic Work

RICHARD PENN SMITH'S DRAMATIC WORK: IMPRINT, MANUSCRIPTS, PRODUCTION

Title, with sources where identifiable	Imprint	Ms. location where known[1]	Production with revival dates when known[2]
The Deformed, or, Woman's Trial [first titled "The Divorce"] from Act II of Thomas Dekker's "The Honest Whore."	Phila., Alexander, 1830	PPHi	Phila., 1830; Rev., 1839, 1846, 1847
The Disowned; or, the Prodigals, from Le Caissier by Jouslin De La Salle	Phila., Alexander, [1830]		Balto., 1829. Rev. 1836, 1847.
The Eighth of January (To celebrate Jackson's victory at New Orleans, 1815.)	Phila., Neal & Mackenzie, 1829		Phila., 1829
Quite Correct, from a story by Theodore Hook, "Doubts and Fears"	In Alexander's Modern Acting Drama, Vol. II, Phila., Carey & Hart, 1835	PPHi	Phila., 1828
Is She a Brigand, by the author's statement, altered from the French Clara Wendel; ou, La Demoiselle Brigand, by Theaulon, et al.	As above, Vol. I		Phila., 1833
Triumph at Plattsburg (To commemorate the great naval battle of War of 1812)	In A.H. Quinn's Representative American Plays, 1917, pp. 165-180	PPHi	Phila., 1830
A Wife at a Venture		PPHi	Phila., 1829
The Sentinels, from Damon and Pythias theme	The Sentinels and Other Plays, Princeton, 1941, reprinted, Indiana U. Press, 1965	PPHi	Phila., 1829
William Penn	Fragment printed and reprinted in The Sentinels, above	PPHI MH	Phila., 1829 Rev. 1842

[1] PPHi: Historical Society of Pennsylvania; MH: Harvard University; PU: University of Pennsylvania.

[2] Dates of initial performances are from McCullough, *The Life and Writings of Richard Penn Smith*. The revival dates are taken, where possible, from Arthur H. Wilson, *A History of the Philadelphia Theatre, 1835–1855*.

Title, with sources where identifiable	Imprint	Ms. location where known[1]	Production with revival dates when known[2]
The Water Witch (Dramatization of Cooper's novel)		MH but not Smith Ms.	Phila., 1830
Caius Marius		PU	Phila., 1831 Rev. 1858
My Uncle's Wedding			Phila., 1832
The Actress of Padua, from *Angelo, Tyran de Padoue,* by Victor Hugo	Phila. Carey & Hart, 1836		Phila., 1836 Rev. 1851, 1852, 1853
The Daughter, from a novel, *Le Siège de La Rochelle* by Mme. de Genlis and *Clara; ou, La Malheur et la Conscience,* by Laroche.	In *The Actress of Padua . . . .,* Phila.; Carey & Hart, 1836	MH	Phila., 1836 Rev. 1837, 1842, 1850
The Bravo (Dramatization of Cooper's novel)		PPHi Fragment at MH titled "The Venetian"	[1836?] Rev. 1849
The Bombardment of Algiers, Tr. of *Le Bombardement d'Alger* by Dupetite-Mère		PPHi	
The Last Man (shows evidence of French sources)		PPHi	
The Pelican (shows evidence of French sources)		PPHI	
Shakespeare in Love, Tr. of Alexandre Duval's *Shakespeare Amoureux*		PPHi	
The Solitary		PPHi	

A Selective Bibliography

ADAMS, THOMAS RANDOLPH. *Trial Check List of the Writings of William Smith, First Provost of the University of Pennsylvania.* Philadelphia, 1950.

Alexander's Modern Acting Drama Consisting of the Most Popular Plays Produced at the Philadelphia Theatre and Elsewhere. 2v. Philadelphia, Carey & Hart, 1935.

ALGER, WILLIAM R. *Life of Edwin Forrest.* 2v. Philadelphia, Lippincott, 1877.

BARRETT, LAWRENCE. *Edwin Forrest.* Boston, Osgood, 1881.

BATES, ALFRED (ed.). *The Drama: its History, Literature and Influence.* . . . (Euripedes Ed.), 20v. London, Athenian Society, 1903.

BRADLEY, E. SCULLEY. *George Henry Boker, Poet and Patriot.* Philadelphia, University of Pennsylvania Press, 1927.

BRIGHAM, CLARENCE S. *History and Bibliography of American Newspapers, 1690–1820.* 2v. Worcester, American Antiquarian Society, 1947.

BROWN, DAVID PAUL. *The Forum; or Forty Years Full Practice at the Philadelphia Bar.* 2v. Philadelphia, Small, 1856.

———. *Sertorius: or, The Roman Patriot. A Tragedy.* Philadelphia, Carey & Hart, 1830.

BROWN, THOMAS ALLSTON. *History of the American Stage.* New York, Dick & Fitzgerald, 1870.

CHENEY, SHELDON. *Stage Decoration.* New York, Day, 1928.

———. *The Theatre: Three Thousand Years of Drama.* . . . New York, Tudor, 1929.

COAD, ORAL SUMNER. *William Dunlap.* . . . (Dunlap Society Publications, Ser. 3, Vol. 2). New York, Dunlap Society, 1917.

Daily Chronicle. Philadelphia.

Dictionary of American Biography. ALLEN JOHNSON, ed., 11v. New York, Scribner's, 1957.

DURANG, CHARLES. *The Philadelphia Stage from the Year 1749 to 1855* (In the *Sunday Dispatch*, 1st ser. 1749-1821, starting in the paper of May 7, 1854; 2nd ser. 1822–1830, starting June 29, 1856; 3rd ser. 1830–1855, starting in the paper July 8, 1860.)

FOOT, JOHN FORRESTER. *A Brief Treatise on the Principles and Advantages of Elocution.* New York, Peabody, 1833.

FREEDLEY, GEORGE. *A History of the Theatre, revised edition, by. . . . and John A. Reeves.* New York, Crown, 1955.

GEGENHEIMER, ALBERT FRANK. "Provost Smith and his group." Philadelphia, 1941. Unpublished doctoral thesis at the University of Pennsylvania.

GODFREY, THOMAS. *Juvenile Poems. . . . with the Prince of Parthia.* Philadelphia, Miller, 1765.

HARRISON, GABRIEL. *Edwin Forrest: The Actor and the Man.* Brooklyn, Eagle Press, 1889.

HAWKINS, F. W. *Life of Edmund Kean.* London, Tinsley, 1869.

HEITLAND, WILLIAM EMERTON. *A Short History of the Roman Republic.* Cambridge, Eng., Cambridge University Press, 1911.

HEWITT, BARNARD. *Theatre U. S. A. 1665 to 1957.* New York, McGraw-Hill, 1959.

HILL, FRANK PIERCE. *American Plays Printed 1714–1830, a Bibliographical Record.* Stanford, Calif., Stanford University Press, 1934.

HORNBLOW, ARTHUR. *A History of the Theatre in America.* 2v. Philadelphia, Lippincott, 1919.

HUGHES, GLENN. *The Story of the Theatre.* New York, French, 1928.

IRELAND, JOSEPH N. *Records of the New York Stage.* 2v. New York, Merrell, 1867.

JAMES, REESE D. *Old Drury of Philadelphia, a History of the Philadelphia Stage 1800-1835. . . .* Philadelphia, University of Pennsylvania Press, 1932.

JONSON, BEN. *The Workes. . . .* London, Bishop, 1640.

LODGE, THOMAS. *The Wounds of Civil War, Lively Set Forth in the True Tragedies of Marius and Scilla.* London, Danter, 1594.

LONG, GEORGE. *Decline of the Roman Republic.* 5v. London, Bell & Daldy, 1864-74.

MABBOTT, THOMAS OLLIVE. "Richard Penn Smith's Tragedy of *Caius Marius,*" *American Literature.* II, 2 (May, 1930), 141-56.

McCULLOUGH, BRUCE WELKER. *The Life and Writings of Richard Penn Smith with a Reprint of His Play, "The Deformed," 1830.* Menasha, Wis., Banta, 1917 (University of Pennsylvania doctoral thesis, 1917).

McKAY, GEORGE L. *American Book Auction Catalogues, 1713–1934.* New York, New York Public Library, 1937.

MICHELET, JULES. *History of the Roman Republic.* London, Bogue, 1847.

MOODY, RICHARD. *Edwin Forrest, First Star of the American Stage.* New York, Knopf, 1960.

MOSES, MONTROSE J. and JOHN MASON BROWN (eds.). *The American Theatre as seen by Its Critics, 1752–1934.* New York, Norton, 1934.

MOSES, MONTROSE J. *The Fabulous Forrest.* Boston, Little, Brown, 1929.

——. *Representative Plays by American Dramatists. . . . 1815–1858.* New York, Dutton, 1925.

MURDOCH, JAMES E. *The Stage or Recollections of Actors and Acting. . . .* Philadelphia, Stoddard, 1880.

NAGLER, A. M. *Sources of Theatrical History.* New York, Theatre Annual, Inc., 1952.

NEW YORK PUBLIC LIBRARY. *The Development of Scenic Art and Stage Machinery . . . Compiled by William Burt Gamble.* New York, New York Public Library, 1920.

NICOLL, ALLARDYCE. *A History of English Drama, 1660–1900.* 6v. Cambridge, Eng., Cambridge University Press, 1923-1959.

OBERHOLTZER, ELLIS PAXSON. *The Literary History of Philadelphia.* Philadelphia, Jacobs, 1906.

ODELL, GEORGE C. C. *Annals of the New York Stage.* 4v. New York, Columbia University Press, 1927-1928.

OTWAY, THOMAS. *The History and Fall of Caius Marius.* London, for Tho. Flesher, 1680.

The New York Clipper.

The New York Dramatic Mirror.

Plutarch's Lives. Translated . . . by John Langhorne and William Langhorne. . . . 4v. Philadelphia, Hickman & Hazzard, 1822.

POTTER, JOHN (Abp. of Canterbury). *Archaeologia graeca, or, the Antiquities of Greece.* 2v. Oxford, Eng., Small, Child, 1967 — 1699.

PROCTOR, B. W. *The Life of Edmund Kean.* 2v. London, Moxon, 1835.

PROCTOR, PAGE S., Jr. "The Life and Works of William Leggett." Unpublished doctoral dissertation at Yale University, 1949.

QUINN, ARTHUR HOBSON. *A History of the American Drama from the Beginning to the Civil War.* 2nd ed., New York, Crofts, 1946.

——. *Representative American Plays.* New York, Century, 1919.

REES, JAMES. *Dramatic Authors of America.* Philadelphia, Zieber, 1845.

——. *Life of Edwin Forrest.* Philadelphia, Peterson, 1874.

RODEN, ROBERT. *Later American Plays, 1831–1900.* New York, Dunlap Society, 1900.

SABIN, JOSEPH. *Bibliotheca Americana: A Dictionary of Books Relating to America, from its Discovery to the Present Time.* 29v. New York, 1868-1936.

San Francisco Bulletin.

SCHARF, J. THOMAS and THOMPSON WESTCOTT. *History of Philadelphia.* 3v. Philadelphia, Everts, 1884.

SCHOENBERGER, HAROLD W. *American Adaptations of French Plays on the New York and Philadelphia Stages from 1790 to 1833.* Philadelphia, Westbrook, 1924.

SIMPSON, HENRY. *The Lives of Eminent Philadelphians.* Philadelphia, Brotherhead, 1859.

SMITH, HORACE WEMYSS. *Life and Correspondence of the Reverend William Smith D. D.* 2v. Philadelphia, George, 1879.

SMITH, IRVINE N. "American Plays and Playwrights of the Nineteenth Century." Unpublished doctoral dissertation at the University of Denver, 1959.

SMITH, RICHARD PENN. *Miscellaneous Works, Collected by his son, Horace W. Smith.* Philadelphia, H.W. Smith, 1856.

SMITH, RICHARD PENN. *The Sentinels and Other Plays,* RALPH

H. WARE and H. W. SCHOENBERGER, Eds. Princeton, N.J., Princeton University Press, 1941.

SMITH, SOL. *Theatrical Management in the West and South for Thirty Years.* New York, Harper, 1868.

SMITH, WILLIAM. *The Collection Books of Provost Smith. . . .* Philadelphia, University of Pennsylvania Press, 1964.

SMITH, WILLIAM MOORE. *Poems, on Several Occasions, Written in Pennsylvania. . . . .* Philadelphia, Story, 1786.

Speech Monographs, XVI, No. 3 (Nov. 1949) "A Bibliography on Theatre and Drama in American Colleges and Universities, 1937-1947."

Spirit of the Times. New York.

STONE, HENRY D. *Personal Recollections of the Drama.* Albany, Van Benthuysen, 1873.

WALKER, JOHN. *A Critical Pronouncing Dictionary.* New York, Collins, 1819.

WATSON, JOHN F. *Annals of Philadelphia. . . .* 3v. Philadelphia, Stuart, 1905.

WEMYSS, FRANCIS COURTNEY. *Twenty-six Years of the Life of an Actor and Manager.* 2v. New York, Burgess, Stringer, 1847.

———. *Wemyss' Chronology of the American Stage from 1752 to 1852.* New York, Taylor, 1852.

WILSON, ARTHUR H. *A History of the Philadelphia Theatre 1835 to 1855.* Philadelphia, University of Pennsylvania Press, 1935.

WINTER, WILLIAM. *Shadows of the Stage.* 2nd ser. New York, Macmillan, 1893.

———. *The Wallet of Time. . . .* 2v. New York, Moffat, Yard, 1918.

WOOD, WILLIAM B. *Personal Recollections of the Stage.* Philadelphia, Baird, 1855.

Index